Journalism's Lost Generation

This book looks at the journalism industry and its changes during the late 20th century and early 21st century. It's a researched and opinionated take on the transitions brought on my television, the internet, and budget declines. Reinardy's underlying theme is that the changes in the industry don't just indicate a newspaper crisis, but also a crisis of local communities, a loss of professional skills, and a void in institutional and community knowledge emanating from newsrooms. *Journalism's Lost Generation* will also document those who remain trying to fill those voids by taking a level view of the newspaper journalism being produced today.

Scott Reinardy is a professor in the William Allen White School of Journalism and Mass Communication at the University of Kansas.

Journalism's Lost Generation
The Un-doing of U.S. Newspaper Newsrooms

Scott Reinardy

Routledge
Taylor & Francis Group

NEW YORK AND LONDON

First published 2017
by Routledge
711 Third Avenue, New York, NY 10017

and by Routledge
2 Park Square, Milton Park, Abingdon, Oxon, OX14 4RN

Routledge is an imprint of the Taylor & Francis Group, an informa business

© 2017 Taylor & Francis

Library of Congress Cataloging in Publication Data
CIP data has been requested.

ISBN: 978-1-138-67499-8 (hbk)
ISBN: 978-1-315-56093-9 (ebk)

Typeset in Times New Roman PS
by diacriTech, Chennai

For Cindy and Trent who encourage, support, and inspire me each day.

For all newspaper journalists who dedicate their lives to serve as watchdogs, guardians, and voices for their communities.

Notation: At their request, names were sometimes changed to protect the identity of journalists still working in newsrooms.

Contents

Preface

The gray-haired general manager had been with the newspaper for more than 30 years when we struck up a conversation in the hallway one afternoon in the mid-1990s.

"What do you think is happening in the newsroom?" he casually asked.

Ownership had hired an outside consulting firm to conduct an assessment of the newsroom staff. They wanted to measure the overall satisfaction and commitment of news workers. Although the general manager had not seen the final report, it was clear he thought any result was an indictment of him and his job.

"I think the morale might be a little low," I said, without giving the words much thought.

Without hesitation, the general manager shot back, "Well, I think poor morale is just bad attitude."

With that, he left me standing alone in the hallway thinking, "We work really hard. We feel underappreciated and demoralized. Our immediate supervisor is a tyrant, and our workload presses us beyond 50 hours a week without overtime pay. And, the paper is exceedingly profitable. Bad attitude? Could management be that callous?"

After a decade of multiple rounds of layoffs, wage freezes, furloughs, budget cuts, an endless workload and new, digital job responsibilities, the answer seems obvious. During an economic downturn, the quickest way to retrieve lost revenue is to cut staff. And in the early 21st century when advertising revenue declined by 55 percent and circulation dropped by 26 percent, that's what newspaper publishers did. In a decade, newspapers eliminated 33 percent of their journalists. Some newsrooms suffered personnel losses as high as 70 percent. The divestment in human capital was devastating to the "layoff survivors" who were committed or simply commissioned to "Keep calm and carry on."

From the newsrooms of small and mid-sized local newspapers (less than 100,000 circulation), hundreds of interviews and conversations tell a story of a dispirited profession depleted in numbers that has lost its sense of purpose. For journalists still committed to producing fair, unbiased, and accurate journalism, there has been a normative failure of newspaper managers and owners to provide a clear mission.

Almost overnight new technology redefined what it meant to be a journalist. Newspapers were the media equivalent of whip and buggy makers to Henry Ford's assembly line of automobiles. The Internet presented a truly open marketplace of ideas unlike any other in human history. Publishers, editors, and reporters were no longer the "deciders" of what was news. The information marketplace was fractured, diminishing news as a social and economic commodity. No longer was publication limited by *The New Yorker*'s A.J. Liebling's "Freedom of the press is guaranteed only to those who own one." In the early 21st century the Internet provided almost every American access to a press. Trained, professional journalists – those who received college degrees to learn the craft – became expendable. They were cynically labeled "The Mainstream Media," as an outdated and out of touch institution with an agenda.

In the aftermath of layoffs, buyouts, and attrition, an army of journalists left newsrooms. Newspaper lifers were no longer considered relevant, or equipped to produce "new" or "multimedia" journalism. The newsroom cuts of seasoned workers decimated institutional and community knowledge, creating a cultural gap of work routines and practices. Ultimately, generations of news workers not only lost jobs but entire careers. Another generation entered a newsroom of turmoil that was struggling to redefine the practice of responsible journalism.

For the newsroom survivors, the sense of purpose and commitment was fundamentally altered as well. The desire to produce quality journalism persisted; however, generating online content and clicks were prioritized. Instead of acting as a community watchdog, journalists had a new charge, one constructed on speed and personal engagement designed to reach new audiences. In the end, what newsroom cuts saved owners in money they lost in community capital. In an effort to cut their way to economic salvation, owners devalued their own newspapers and the journalists who produced it.

This work is an examination of news workers who remain committed to professional newspaper journalism. The research that includes data from more than 5,000 daily newspaper journalists delves inside the psyche of an institution protected by the First Amendment that persevered during the rise of radio and television, and was transformed in light of new technologies. It's a critical examination of how newspaper journalism is being conducted by those still bound by the sense of commitment to inform and educate their communities. It's a story of a lost generation of news workers caught between two journalistic worlds; one of traditional news values, and another perpetuated by Internet content and social media initiatives. The layoff survivors work in a newsroom environment that has left them confused and fearful for their profession. The loss is personal, and for some, tragic.

1 The Collapse

Newspaper newsrooms of the early 21st century were brimming with personnel. Mid-sized newspapers (between 50,001–100,000 circulation) routinely supported staffs of 120 or more. What would be unimaginable jobs today (religion reporter, fashion writer, and special projects teams) were routine and even promoted on local billboards and television commercials.

The long-standing formula for newspaper staff size was one journalist for every 1,000 daily papers sold (Meyer and Minjeong, 2002; Robertson, 2002). During the 1990s, many mid-sized newspapers had a ratio of 1.5 or 2 journalists for every 1,000 sales (Robertson, 2002). By 2001, newspaper journalists numbered more than 56,000–11,000 more than just two decades earlier. Employment remained steady for the next few years, with few indications of what was to come.

In 2007, Erica Smith was a *St. Louis Post-Dispatch* news designer. Less than a decade into her journalism career, she had a general curiosity about the news industry, and noticed a shift. Employment of newspaper journalists still hovered at about 55,000, but a few of her friends had been laid off. She also began reading briefs about large papers cutting staff. At first, Smith compiled a simple list of newspaper layoffs but then came a larger purpose. Actually, two larger purposes.

With news content shifting to the Internet, Smith realized she needed to bolster her skill set. She wanted to learn Web development. Tracking newspaper layoffs on a website provided an opportunity. Additionally, Smith could fill a need for those curious about the job losses.

In mid-2007, Smith launched "Papercuts." The interactive U.S. map was stuck with colorful pins that listed the name of the newspaper making the cut, ownership group, date of cuts, how many jobs lost (in the newsroom and throughout the newspaper) and sometimes a note about the layoff. By 2008, the map was covered in different colored pins indicating the size of the cuts (white = 1–24; yellow = 25–49; blue = 50–74, etc.). Net job losses in 2008 totaled nearly 16,000 by Smith's count. The map was again covered in pins in 2009 as more than 14,000 jobs were lost.

Smith admits there wasn't anything scientific about her count. She was an aggregator merely plotting information she either gathered or was provided. In fact, on many occasions she said her count probably wasn't accurate. "It's impossible to say exactly how many people lost their jobs," she said in a 2015 interview. "A lot of newspapers didn't report it." Nonetheless, she became the expert, fulfilling media interview requests asking about the numbers. Smith admits she had few answers when asked, "What does it mean?" or "Where will the industry go from here?" She mostly avoided issuing analysis, saying her opinions about the future of newspapers carried little validity.

Meanwhile through Papercuts, Smith's Web and social media skills grew. She became a *Post-Dispatch* multimedia producer and eventually the social media editor. The new titles provided more job security for Smith. The *P-D* went through its own rounds of layoffs. Per protocol, Smith mapped those as well. But sticking colored pins on an electronic map, some of which represented friends and colleagues, had a price. In a blog post on Nov. 7, 2010, Smith wrote: "I'm tired of updating Paper Cuts. There's a whole lot more layoffs to add tomorrow. (I shall wear a tiara while adding to the layoff total in an effort to fend off newspaper depression)."

In a 2015 interview, Smith admitted that "newspaper depression" was just part of it. "Some days I'd work on it and I just couldn't take it anymore. Other days it was, 'I was just putting the numbers together.' It always came back to telling the story. But it was definitely heartbreaking at times."

As a union newsroom, the layoff protocol at the *Post-Dispatch* was "last one in; first one out." In the event of layoffs, those hired most recently lost their jobs first. Although Smith's tenure at the paper was less than some, she received a layoff reprieve at least on one occasion. The union contract afforded an exemption for an employee with special or unique skills. During one layoff, Smith was the only person coordinating social media. Because of her special skills, she was exempt from the layoff but realized it was a temporary reprieve. "I knew my time was coming."

So on April 13, 2012, Smith left the *Post-Dispatch* on her own terms. She began working for Infuz, a digital marketing agency. By the end of 2012, Smith had taken on so many projects that something had to give. It would be Papercuts. At the time she blogged: "In April 2012, I left the *St. Louis Post-Dispatch* and the newspaper industry. After a couple of months off from this website, I'm now working on catching up. The map will be updated last; the total is current. Tips and questions are always welcome: newspaperlayoffs@gmail.com. Thanks."

"I wish I hadn't stopped working on the site," Smith admitted in 2015. "... People still email me to this day about being laid off. There was overwhelming support for keeping track of the information and not just keeping track of the big papers. Being laid off at the small paper had just as much impact for those journalists as those working at big papers."

Although Smith never became a pin on her Papercuts map, she was eventually laid off from a non-newspaper job. Nine months after becoming the Curator in Chief at the online aggregation news website RealTime/STL, Smith lost her job. "Just like newspapers, we couldn't figure out the business model," she said. Smith quickly caught on as an online producer for St. Louis Public Radio.

All told, between 2007–11, Smith recorded 40,224 layoffs and buyouts on her Papercuts map. Although the map is still available under "Newspaperlayoffs.com," it's frozen in 2012, listing 1,859+ jobs lost because of layoffs or buyouts at U.S. newspapers. She said she hopes to someday return to the map but for now most of the connected links ring up "404" errors. The final pin Smith stuck in the map was red, indicating 100 or more cuts. It read:

> *The Cincinnati Enquirer*
> Owner: Gannett Co. Inc.
> Date: October, 2012
> Layoffs: 200
> Printing will be outsourced to *The Columbus Dispatch*.

Smith's work chronicled a time when newspaper employment went from a thriving occupation to an endangered workforce. In just a few years, thousands who felt destined to be news lifers until retirement or death became the unemployed and unemployable middle-aged. Almost overnight, how they did their work became obsolete. Coupled with the "Great Recession" of the mid-2000s, the veteran newspaper journalist was expensive and, ultimately, expendable.

By 2014, the job of newspaper reporter was on CareerCast's most endangered jobs list. In summarizing the selection, CareerCast wrote: "Declining subscription and dwindling advertising sales have negatively impacted the hiring power of some newspapers, while others have ceased operations altogether. Online outlets continue to replace traditional newspapers, and the long-term outlook for newspaper reporters reflects the change."

CareerCast reports that by 2022, hiring projections for newspaper reporters was −13 percent. Only mail carriers (−28 percent), meter readers (−19 percent) and farmers (−19 percent) have worse job prospects. (CareerCast, 2014).

By 2014, the number of newspaper journalists had dropped to about 37,000–5,000 fewer than in 1978, according to the American Society of News Editors. Almost overnight, newsrooms became ghost towns. The empty desks strewn throughout the newsroom were tombstone reminders of what once was in American journalism. The newspaper apocalypse of the mid-2000s eviscerated newsrooms by about 33 percent. In light of sharp declines in advertising revenue (55 percent) and circulation (26 percent), newspaper owners purged news staffs in an effort to balance the books.

What owners saved in money they lost in community capital. Newsrooms now operate with skeleton staffs, expected to produce a steady stream of local news and information. Those hefty newsrooms of 120 or more now house half that or fewer journalists. The staffers who remain carry several titles and multiple job responsibilities. Pay cuts and furloughs are commonplace. For the news worker, the sense of purpose and commitment has been shredded. The idea of providing quality journalism is a wistful notion. The time crunch and additional workload are obstacles in producing investigative, analytical, or in-depth journalism.

There was a time when newspapers mattered. They were the lifeblood for people seeking jobs, a new set of tires, or a good story about a boy and his dog. Newspapers informed the voters about elected officials, tax spending, bond issues, and crime. Newspapers offered readers a place to remember the deceased, commemorate our history, celebrate anniversaries and births, shout from the editorial page, and cheer our sports teams.

Newspapers employed reporters and editors who sorted information into digestible nuggets. Readers left it to the professionals to determine the importance of news. The newspaper could be trusted to tell its readers what really mattered. And in that, the process was flawed. Reporters and editors propagated influence and bias. They set the agenda, deciding who had a voice and who did not. The *New York Times*' "All the News That's Fit to Print" clearly identifies who decides what is news. Sure, there were mistakes, but accountability was trivialized. While mishaps occurred under large, front-page headlines, corrections were an afterthought, tucked deep inside the paper under the small, unnoticeable title "Corrections."

It was an imperfect system. What was protected by the First Amendment became a shield, and a weapon. Under that protection, reporters attacked corruption and injustice, or a new box store that was destined to strangle Main Street. Newspapers were the guardians of the community. The local paper carried gravitas when it backed a political candidate or printed a full-page American flag on Memorial Day or rallied around the high school football team. The editors and reporters published what they christened important or necessary or profitable to their needs. There was power in the press. And there was a sense of pride to work at the local newspaper.

As with many drawn to journalism, Kiyoshi Martinez was all in. He earned a bachelor's degree (University of Illinois-Urbana) and a master's in journalism (University of Illinois-Springfield). As an undergrad he had been a reporter, columnist, and editor-in-chief at *The Daily Illini*. But by the time Martinez was 23 he was out. He had quit his newspaper job to become a communications specialist for an Illinois politician. Even as a young journalist, Martinez felt the newspaper landscape shift.

"I really like journalism and had a lot of fun doing it, but I was thinking about where I was going to be after my first job," he said in 2008. "Would I still be in the industry 10 years from now? I reached the conclusion that it wasn't a place for me, and it wasn't very stable."

Martinez's final job in a newsroom was as a Web editor for 22nd Century Media, publishers of more than a dozen hyper-local weekly newspapers. "I didn't see myself doing the *All the President's Men*, Woodward and Bernstein journalism that they kind of pump you up on in J-school. I didn't see the point in sticking around in a job where eight hours a day doing something that's completely mind-numbing."

As he was departing 22nd Century Media in 2008, Martinez began to think about the long-time plight of newspapers and their journalists. Were other newsies just as frustrated? Admittedly, frustration among newspaper folk is not an anomaly. Equally as common is finding a journalist willing to vent about his or her frustration.

For Martinez, the Internet could allow the grumbling to move from the barroom to the public domain. So in February 2008, Martinez launched "AngryJournalist.com." Although the newsroom downsizing was just beginning, the fifth post on the site read: "Oh, if only I could FIND a journalism job. F' downsizing and recessions."

Angry Journalist No. 6 responded: "Oh, you'll find one, and then you'll realize the only reason you got it is because you're the only whore who will work for that low of a salary. And then when the other people who work with you quit, they'll give you a 17 percent raise and a 50 percent workload increase for as long as they possibly can. Fuck the publishers, guys. Fuck 'em."

And so it began. Within a year, nearly 8,000 angry journalists had posted to the website. "I feel a lot of it is venting, but I think it's worse now just because it's depressing to read industry news," Martinez said in 2008. "I don't think it's so much anger, it's a sense of despair and depression that, 'Yeah, maybe I'm not getting laid off but where am I going to go next?'"

Although Martinez's site closed after a few years, the anger, despair, frustration, and career depression were just taking hold. Papercuts and AngryJournalist were simply precursors. Perpetuated by the Great Recession, the tsunami of layoffs, buyouts, and dismantling of newsrooms was just beginning. And when the tsunami subsided, the newsroom culture and the ideology of producing news and information were fundamentally changed. Institutional and community knowledge was lost. News was now measured in clicks and Web traffic and unique visitors. Producing news for the newspaper was one thing. Producing news for the digital world was something altogether different.

The veteran staffer soon discovered all that passion and incentive for becoming a journalist no longer applied. What they were being asked to do rarely resembled the journalism of their youths. Even those who didn't lose their jobs were forever transformed. Many became the bridge between the old and new journalism, adapting as necessary. Meanwhile, others became a lost generation of journalists.

References

CareerCast (2014). Most endangered jobs of 2014. www.careercast.com/jobs-rated/most-endangered-jobs-2014.

Meyer, P., and Minjeong, K. (2002). How many news people does a newspaper need? Presented to the Newspaper Division, Association for Education in Journalism and Mass Communication, Miami Beach, Fla., August 7.

Robertson, L. (2002). Rule of what? *American Journalism Review*, July/August.

2 Stress and Burnout

After a 25-year career, Reni Winter was reluctant to admit she worked in newspapers. She didn't list her journalism experience on her Facebook or LinkedIn profiles. She didn't stay in contact with former colleagues at the *Lafayette (Ind.) Journal and Courier*. She didn't even like to talk about what once was a passionate career, one she thought she'd never leave. "I so passionately loved my work I never would have thought that I would burnout," Reni admitted in 2010. "I was always the person, 'Give me another story; give me more work. The harder the better.' I loved it."

During the early stages of the Great Newspaper Exodus in the mid-2000s, the work environment began to shift for Reni. In 2007, she felt devalued as the pressure to produce online content mounted. Creativity was supplanted by process, assembly-line journalism. "I had seen myself as a wordsmith … and ended up feeling like something who was more of a machine." "Online first" superseded the doorstep morning edition. New, young hires made her feel antiquated. "I didn't feel I was a writer or an editor anymore. The craft was gone. … I started re-evaluating my identity. Who am I as a journalist?"

After some encouragement, Reni approached the newspaper's human resources manager to discuss what she suspected was burnout. After taking a few minutes to explain her condition, Reni received her answer. "When I saw her reaction I thought, 'My goose is cooked.' All she said was, 'That's not good.' The biggest thing I felt was totally and completely isolated."

By early 2008, layoffs were rippling through the newspaper industry, and the Gannett-owned *Journal and Courier* could not escape the rolling tide. The encounter with HR only exacerbated Reni's work stress. "I started to feel afraid. I wasn't going to be getting any help and it was being viewed as a negative that I shared that. I was on the radar. When talks started the following year of layoffs corporate-wide, I started getting ready."

Along with ten others at the newspaper, including two in the newsroom, Reni was laid off in December 2008. A career dream that started when she was 8 years old, and guided her through a college degree and decades of dedicated work, was over in an instant. "There was a grief process: 'Well, they don't need me anymore.'"

Burnout's Early Years

Although the term "burnout" has seeped into our everyday work vernacular, that wasn't always the case. In the mid-1970s when University of California-Berkeley social psychologists Christina Maslach and Susan Jackson first scientifically explored the notion of burnout, it was classified as "pop psychology." Editors of academic journals repeatedly rejected their study of human service professionals, which included police, counselors, teachers, nurses, social workers, psychiatrists, psychologists, attorneys, physicians, and agency administrators. "It's been a long haul and it's funny because people will introduce me at conferences as a 'pioneer,'" Maslach said in 2010. "I'm thinking, 'Folks, you don't know what it's like when you're all alone and people are not giving you the time of day, much less any respect for any of your ideas.' You're thinking, 'Maybe I just totally don't understand this.'"

The premise of burnout derives from the early 20th century when "to burn oneself out" was English slang meaning "to work too hard and die early" (Partridge, 1950: 111). The term was popularized by Graham Greene's 1960 best-selling novel *A Burnt-Out Case*. In the novel, an African named Deo Gratias had lost his fingers and toes to leprosy. Greene writes, "His toeless feet looked like rods, and when he walked it was as though he was engaged in pounding the path flat" (p. 13). Because the leprosy had eaten away all that it wanted, Deo Gratias is declared cured by Dr. Colin. To allow Deo Gratias to stay on at the colony, Dr. Colin assigns him to assist Querry, the book's main character and a world-famous New York architect seeking to escape his past by venturing to Africa. When Dr. Colin is asked about assigning Deo Gratis to Querry, he said, "He's cured, but he's a burnt-out case and I don't want to send him away. He can sweep a floor or make a bed without fingers and toes" (p. 18).

The physical disabilities that create Deo Gratis' "burnout" correlate with Querry's psychological state of burnout. At one point in the novel, Querry writes in his journal, "I haven't enough feeling left for human beings to do anything for them out of pity ... A vocation is an act of love: it is not a professional career. When desire is dead one cannot continue to make love. I've come to the end of desire and to the end of a vocation" (Greene, 1960: 57).

More than a decade after Greene's novel, psychologist Herbert J. Freudenberger adopted a scholarly approach to burnout. Born in Frankfurt, Germany, in 1926, Freudenberger escaped the Nazis using his father's passport when he was 13, ultimately arriving in New York. He earned his doctorate in psychology from New York University, and had a practice in Manhattan for 40 years. Freudenberger lobbied to establish free clinics for substance abusers in the city, and after a full day at the office, he would work with addicts in East Harlem late into the night. During his career, he analyzed Charles Manson, wrote about the Beatles, and appeared on *Oprah* (Martin, 1999).

Initiated by his own feelings of exhaustion, fatigue, frequent headaches, sleeplessness, and series of other ailments, Freudenberger in 1974 published "Staff Burn-Out" in the *Journal of Social Issues*. Relying upon a dictionary definition of burnout as "to fail, wear out, or become exhausted by making excessive demands on energy, strength, or resources" (p. 159), Freudenberger categorized behavioral signs such as irritation, frustration, and anger. Observing workers at a free clinic, he wrote of those who were burned out: "A greater and greater number of physical hours are spent there, but less and less is being accomplished" (p. 161).

According to Freudenberger, dedicated, committed workers, particularly in the health-care profession, are most susceptible to burnout. Job pressures, long workdays, uncertain organizational goals, minimal organizational support, and job monotony are among the stressors that lead to burnout. "We would rather put up than shut up," he wrote. "And what we put up is our talents, our skills, we put in long hours with a bare minimum of financial compensation. But it is precisely because we are dedicated that we walk into a burn-out trap" (p. 161). Freudenberger's work was the catalyst for burnout research, and he is credited with coining the phrase "burnout" in the work sense. After a career of working 15-hour days, six days a week, Freudenberger died of heart complications in 1999 (Martin, 1999). He was 73.

On the heels of Freudenberger's work, Maslach and Jackson stumbled across the term "burnout" while conducting research on workplace emotions among health care professionals in the mid-1970s. They wanted to better understand how during crises, workers controlled their emotional arousal but remained detached from patients. In a serendipitous conversation with poverty lawyers describing their work, the researchers learned that legal service lawyers experienced a similar phenomenon as health care workers. The lawyers called it "burnout" (Maslach and Jackson, 1984).

Maslach and Jackson's early contributions identified a multifaceted concept of burnout that led to the development of a measureable, standardized three-scale instrument—emotional exhaustion; depersonalization; and personal accomplishment (Maslach and Jackson, 1981). Each measurement included a linking component that either exacerbated or dispelled a condition of burnout. They included:

- Emotional exhaustion: A feeling of being emotionally overextended and depleted of emotional resources.

- Depersonalization: Having a negative or callous feeling and being detached from the people who rely upon your service or assistance.
- Personal accomplishment: A reduction in feelings of competence and achievement from your work (Maslach, 1993, p. 21).

In a sense, the three aspects of burnout create a tumbling effect: emotional exhaustion eventually leads to depersonalization, which will diminish feelings of personal accomplishment. As a worker becomes less invested and less engaged, individual achievement is diminished.

Highly motivated, dedicated individuals enter a profession with the expectation of making a difference. They set goals and enter work environments where others have similar aspirations. Work lives and personal lives blend: "If my work makes a difference, I make a difference" (Pines, 1993, p. 36). It harkens to the age-old question, "What is the meaning of life?" Pines (1993) wrote: "For most burned-out professionals, work initially provided (or was expected to provide) an answer. They knew why they were put on earth: to do the work for which they had a calling" (p. 39). Over time, if failure to fulfill their mission persisted, workers felt as if they were unable to provide significant contributions. Making a difference was no longer possible, feasible, or achievable. At that point, workers become susceptible to burnout (Pine, 1993).

Interestingly, popular culture played a role in the early perception of burnout. Network situation comedies such as *Taxi* (Reverend Jim) and *WKRP in Cincinnati* (Dr. Johnny Fever) included a resident "burnout" character who was disheveled in what was personified as a drug-induced stupor or caused by long-term drug abuse. By the early 1980s, mainstream perception shifted from a drug-addled burnout to people experiencing burnout in an exhaustive work sense. "Because it has a catchy ring to it," Maslach and Jackson wrote in 1984, "burnout is sometimes immediately dismissed as a fad, or as pseudoscientific jargon that is all surface flash and no substance. This negative reaction to the term itself has led some scholars to reject the concept outright and to ignore the research entirely" (p. 139).

Since it's development in 1981, the Maslach Burnout Inventory had been used in thousands of studies, many of which examined workers in people-oriented, helping professions. In 1996, Maslach, Jackson, and Michael Leiter developed the MBI-General Survey, modifying the scale that measured workers in other professions. The three-scale MBI-GS—exhaustion, cynicism, and professional efficacy—"defines burnout as a crisis in one's relationship with work, not necessarily as a crisis in one's relationships with people at work" (Maslach et al., 1996, p. 20). While the MBI emphasized a worker's relationship with people, the MBI-GS examines work performance in general.

Exhaustion measured work fatigue, cynicism examined "indifference or a distant attitude toward work," and professional efficacy examined accomplishments and expectations of work (Maslach et al., 1996, p. 21).

Burnout Among Newspaper Journalists

Although there was a flood of burnout research conducted in the late 1970s and early 1980s, it was Maslach and Jackson's burnout scale that launched a profusion of inquiry that has continued for four decades. By the 35th anniversary of the Maslach Burnout Inventory, Schaufeli, Leiter, and Maslach (2009) estimated that more than 6,000 books, chapters, dissertations, and journal articles about burnout had been published.

Nonetheless, little burnout work among American newspaper journalists had been conducted. A few 1990s studies identified young, entry-level copy editors working at small newspapers as being most susceptible to burnout. (Cook and Banks, 1993; Cook, Banks, and Turner, 1993; Craig, 1999). Cook and Banks wrote that the most at-risk journalist for burnout "expresses intentions to leave the field, has found journalism to be much different from what was expected and demonstrates a low overall level of job satisfaction" (1993: 116).

There was an obvious void in burnout research among newspaper journalists, one I've spent more than a decade trying to fill. My explorations have measured the burnout levels of more than 5,000 newspaper news workers, at 150 daily newspapers from all regions of the U.S. ranging in circulation from 5,000 to more than 1 million. In my research, Maslach's burnout scales were used to measure degrees of burnout, but more importantly, the research explored the causes (workload and support from the organization) and effect (job satisfaction and perception of work quality) of the rising tide of burnout. And that tide is rising.

For burnout to occur, researchers contend workers need to score high on the exhaustion scale, and high on one of the other two scales (Brenninkmeijer and Van Yperen, 2003; Roelofs et al., 2005). Under those guidelines, in 2009, 42 percent (sample size = 2,159) of surviving newspapers journalists in my studies were experiencing some degree of burnout. By 2014, the number had risen to 56 percent (sample size = 1,686), higher than U.S. physicians (46 percent), nurses (43 percent), and medical students (40 percent) (Krupa, 2012; Aiken et al., 2002; Dyrbye et al., 2014) (see Table 1).

Digging deeper, "classic burnout cases" were identified as news workers who scored high on exhaustion and cynicism. Essentially, these were journalists who had reached a demarcation for being burned out. Using this criteria, journalists were more burned out than police officers, air traffic controllers, and construction managers (Richardsen and Martinussen, 2005).

Table 1 Burnout Percentage by Profession

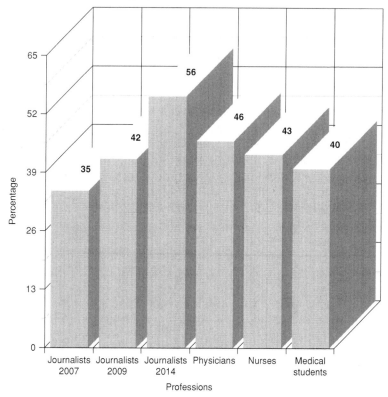

For perspective, consider the case of Air Force drone pilots based in Creech Air Force Base, Nevada, flying sorties into war-torn countries such as Iraq and Afghanistan. A 2014 Government Accountable Office report said the Air Force estimated that 1,600 pilots were needed to maintain the required 65 combat air patrols (CAP) each day. One CAP is a 24-hour Predator drone surveillance mission. When the report was issued, drone pilots were quitting at an alarming rate, and recruiting goals for 2012 and 2013 came up short. The lack of pilots increased the workload and work hours for those on active duty (Government Accountability Office, 2014). By June 2015, the U.S. Air Force reduced the number of CAPs to 60 because stress was burning out drone pilots. A retired Predator drone pilot told *The New York Times* the work was "brutal, 24 hours a day, 365 days a year" (Drew and Philipps, 2015).

No one will contend that newspaper journalists experience the same work pressures as drone pilots. Regardless of profession, comparing work stress among different jobs is a complicated proposition. Multiple factors such as training, types of stress (internal vs. external), and duration of stressors play a role. But just in raw numbers, newspaper journalists surveyed in 2014 (30 percent) were experiencing more burnout than drone pilots (less than 20 percent) (Chappelle et al., 2014).

The number of burned out newspaper journalists spiked at the cusp of newspaper layoffs in 2007 when 37 percent of the study's participants were classic burnout cases (high exhaustion and cynicism). The number dropped to 24 percent in 2009, but rose to 30 percent by 2014. The trend followed an organizational path of instability through a resettlement resulting in a younger and much smaller newsroom staff (see Table 2).

Traditionally, exhaustion has been the catalyst for burnout, acting as a domino that causes high degrees of cynicism and low levels of professional efficacy—a burnout buffer of sorts (Maslach et al., 2001). Since the MBI's inception, the events have been sequential—exhaustion to cynicism to

Table 2 Classic Burnout Cases in Reinardy Studies

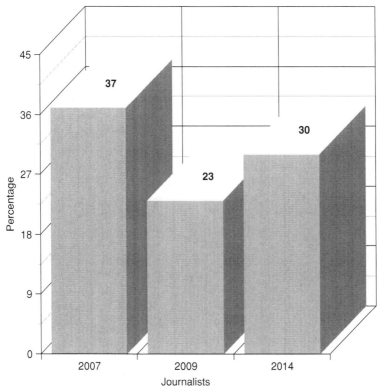

diminished professional efficacy. However, exhaustion is not simply a physical concept but an emotional and cognitive separation from work. The work itself depletes energy and enthusiasm (Maslach et al., 2001). The emotional toll creates feelings of "helplessness, hopelessness, and entrapment" (Schaufeli and Enzmann, 1998: 32). Journalists have not reached a high level of exhaustion.

In fact, between 2007 and 2009 exhaustion actually declined. While it remained in the "average" range, journalists in 2009 reported significantly lower levels of exhaustion than those in 2007, a circumstance that could be attributed to the number of staff layoffs and voluntary departures – many of which were workers already experiencing high degrees of burnout, or at least exhaustion.

While exhaustion had not been a great contributor to journalists' burnout, cynicism had. The MBI-GS' cynicism measurement scale examines the idea that workers are disengaged with the work and begin to question their work lives or the purpose of their work. Passion and dedication begin to wane. Producing journalism—good or otherwise—has been devalued. At the very least, workers adopt a laissez-faire attitude toward work. At the very most, a worker's attitude is so corrosive it disrupts the work of others, and creates a toxic work environment.

From 2007 to 2009, cynicism among journalists in my studies spiked into Maslach's Burnout Inventory high range and held steady through 2014. Cynicism continued to hover in the high range, indicating journalists no longer felt as engaged and committed to their work. Although exhaustion has traditionally been the catalyst for initiating burnout, other studies have seen cynicism take root first. While physical and emotional overload is the mark of exhaustion, cynicism elevates burnout into a stage of disengagement (Schaufeli and Enzmann, 1998).

In a conversation with MBI-GS co-developer Christina Maslach in 2010, she said it's not unusual for cynicism to rise even if exhaustion does not. "For me, one of the issues becomes what is the nature of the job and the kind of work that you do," she said. "Early on, there were real variations between different groups of people. For some, cynicism really shoots up and for others it doesn't. Is that a function of the kind of work you're doing, the kind of training or preparation you've had to handle the work?

"It still raises the question that having that passion for your work or compassion for other people is a good thing in terms in going into the work," she said. "But, as with many things in life, it has a plus and a minus. Does it conceivably provide more of a risk factor?"

Throughout my newsroom studies, professional efficacy has remained consistently in the average range. In general terms that means news workers' feelings of accomplishments and to some degree satisfaction have remained constant. It also says that journalists remain confident in the work they do, and they retain some degree of job satisfaction.

The Face of Burnout

Burnout has many faces. For newsroom workers, burnout crosses the boundaries of gender, age, job description, and professional experience. Nonetheless, the data collected during the past decade have revealed patterns. For instance, between 2007 and 2014, classic burnout cases (high exhaustion and cynicism) continued to rise among older journalists (over 40), with a spike for those between 51–60 by 2014.

By 2009, many of those experiencing burnout had left the newsroom. So while the average age of news workers remained steady (42 to 44 years old) from 2007 to 2009, years working at their current newspaper dropped from 18 to 13, indicating that some older workers changed jobs in that two-year span. Job change had not diminished the climbing rate of burnout. While the environment changed for some burned out journalists, the working conditions—heavy, stressful workloads and new, unfamiliar job responsibilities—had not. Burnout baggage was transitory from one newsroom to another, indicating that stress-related practices are somewhat universal.

Burnout among women was also on the rise. The conflict between work and family among women continued to play a primary factor in job burnout. In traditional gender roles, women prioritize family and home over work obligations, while men assume the role of breadwinners. Newspapers, which traditionally had been a male-dominated profession—particularly among top management—had done little to accommodate women. In 2007, 32 percent of women were experiencing classic burnout (high exhaustion and cynicism) compared with 38 percent men. In 2009 while classic burnout among women rose slightly (34 percent), it dropped exponentially for men (18 percent) (see Table 3).

By 2014, burnout was pushing women to the brink of leaving the profession. In a sample of more than 500 newswomen, 37 percent were suffering classic burnout. Among those with classic burnout, 82 percent said they expected to leave the profession or answered "don't know" to the question, "Do you have any intention of leaving newspaper journalism?" In a sample of about 1,100 men, 25 percent were classic burnout cases in 2014, and of those, 31 percent answered "yes" or "don't know" to the leaving question.

After two years as a city reporter at a mid-size daily, 24-year-old Lori was in the "don't know" category. She was frustrated with the newspaper's slow transition from the print product to digital, and said online work was merely a replication of the print product. The paper had undergone several rounds of layoffs, and morale was low.

Table 3 Classic Burnout of Men vs. Women in Reinardy Studies

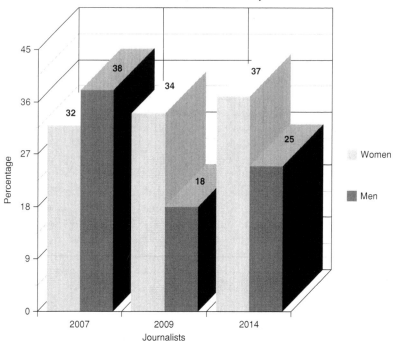

"I'd say our staff is grumpy and disgruntled," Lori said in 2014. "There's a lot of griping, 'I don't get to do what I want and I am being told what to do today.' A lot of people that work here have seen a lot of people get laid off, have not had a raise in years, have seen multiple owners of the newspaper and their different styles."

As veteran workers reminisced about the "good old days," they worked under the pale of more layoffs and a reduction in resources. Once when a staff meeting was announced, fear engulfed the newsroom. "Everyone expected the worst," Lori said. "It's like a shelter dog where you can't turn on the hose without him running away."

As with most in her newsroom, Lori was uncertain of its future, and hers, but said the staff remained dedicated to producing good work.

> Everyone that works here is here because they want to be here. If they wanted a career that offers job security they probably wouldn't be here. If they wanted a career that gives them a 2 percent raise each year, they

Table 4 Classic Burnout by Age in Reinardy Studies

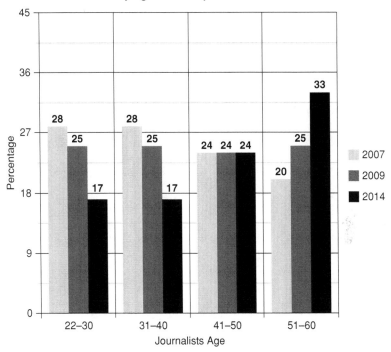

wouldn't be here. I think the people that are here do believe in what we do and the service we provide to the community. That being said, there's a lot of fear inside the newsroom.

Notable in my 2014 research was that journalists with the least amount of professional experience (less than 5 years) and the most experience (more than 21 years) accounted for the bulk of classic burnout cases. Burnout among less experienced workers was not unexpected. New to the workload and the expectations of a full-time journalism job created unfamiliar stress on novice journalists, leading to burnout. The same did not necessarily hold true for veteran news workers. A logical conclusion was that the daily grind had finally taken its toll. Along with job insecurity, journalists who once thought they'd retire from the newspaper were no longer sure that would be possible (see Table 4).

Reporters in 2014 were showing signs of classic burnout more than any other job title in the newsroom. Reporters were on the front lines of

Table 5 Classic Burnout by Job Title in Reinardy 2014 Study

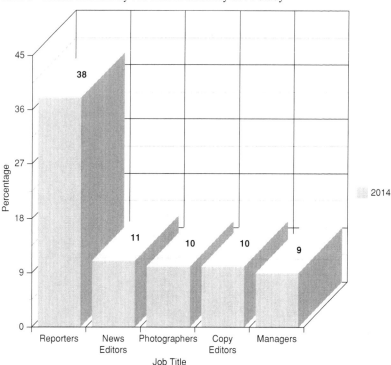

newsroom changes. When staffs were cut, reporters assumed the responsibility of multiple beats. When newsroom management implemented online and social media initiatives, reporters were generating the additional content. The trial and error of information creation primarily fell to reporters. The workload stress was compounded by the frustration of failed or soon-to-be abandoned efforts (see Table 5).

Andy was a 16-year veteran reporter who survived several rounds of layoffs and an ownership change at his mid-sized newspaper. He understood the economics of the industry but said, "They cut our staff to the bare bones. When I first came here, that whole room was full. The size of the newsroom has been crushed."

A large portion of the newsroom featured an expanse of beige carpet where dozens of cubicles used to be. Andy had not only absorbed some of the work from those who have been laid off but added tweeting, blogging, and posting videos to his daily workload. "People rush so much now to get things online we're not even sure if we're right," he said. "I don't think it matters so much if it's right; I think it matters that you're first."

What weighed even more heavily on Andy was his future. After 16 dedicated years at the newspaper, he had little job security. "I have no doubt that I'm going to lose my job someday. There's no doubt in my mind that I'm going to come in here after 18 or 20 years and they're going to walk me out."

In the meantime, Andy said he would continue to absorb more work, question the quality of that work, and hope for the sake of his family he could prolong the day he was escorted from the newsroom by security.

> I have a wife and kids and a mortgage. You do what you have. Life goes on. What am I supposed to do: whine and cry? If they're going to let us go, it's not because I'm doing a good or bad job. It's going to be because of money.

Context

Stress has always been an underlying job condition of newspaper journalism. Work conditions are rife with a copious number of stressors, among them deadlines, competition, and workload. In recent years, stressors have been compounded by new and different work responsibilities, online production, social media work, and an unrelenting 24/7/365 news cycle flush with competition from traditional media and non-traditional information sources.

Stressors lead to stress, and stress is at the core of burnout. But stress is also a necessary and acceptable part of life. College graduates stress about job prospects; business owners stress about making payroll; parents stress over their children's health. Stress is unrelenting and problematic for some. Meanwhile, others thrive under its presence. Each person learns to adapt and cope with life and work stress in different ways.

Not all stress is bad. Stress adds variety and excitement to our lives. While stress for one person is invigorating, the same stress can make another person physically ill. Stress can also be simultaneously good and bad—a promotion with a pay raise is exciting; the new job responsibilities are unnerving. The difference lies in how each individual copes with stress.

Because work relationships are similar to personal relationships, workers will endure stressful times with the expectation that there will be a beneficial outcome. If stress levels exceed a person's capability to cope, it can lead to unhappiness, dissatisfaction, reduction in work performance, and even illness (Lazarus and Launier, 1978; Brill, 1984). During high degrees of stress, some people will adapt, stabilize, and perhaps even improve their performance, but for those who reach the burnout level, there is little redemption (Maslach et al., 2001).

Early in burnout research, Maslach and others determined that once burnout takes hold a worker's options are limited. Removing a worker from the job or altering individual coping strategies might help but they do not address situational or organizational factors, which play a larger role in creating burnout than individual actions (Maslach, Schaufeli, and Leiter, 2001). Maslach et al. (2001) wrote:

> People may be able to tolerate greater workload if they value the work and feel they are doing something important, or if they feel well-rewarded for their efforts, and so an intervention could target these areas of value and reward (p. 419).

Stress-related issues can be devastating to individuals and organizations. Stress sufferers miss on average 23 workdays a year (Webster and Bergman, 1999). Job stress that results in accidents, absenteeism, turnover, reduced productivity, medical and insurance costs, and workers' compensation cost U.S. businesses more than $300 billion annually (The American Institute of Stress, 2006).

But what is a newspaper journalism job if not stressful? It's a badge of honor among journalists to proclaim, "I work better under stress." Stress is the fire that burns red-hot when chasing the next story, locating and correcting errors in stories on deadline, and putting the paper to bed moments after the final story is filed. Stress is the scratchy noise screeching from a police scanner that sends a cop reporter racing from the newsroom, a city editor orchestrating coverage of a train derailment, and a designer remaking A1 22 minutes before the press begins to whirl.

Well, that's how it used to be. The newspaper world changed. Reductions in news staff has layoff survivors doing more with less at an accelerated pace. With fewer veteran staffers, there are fewer who instill calm during stressful times. The veterans are finding themselves overburdened and cynical of the work. The young staffers are learning through trial and error.

For 37 years Ann had worked a variety of jobs at the same newspaper. The on-the-job lessons she learned were taught by gruff editors who demanded high quality, and weren't afraid to express their displeasure. Now, she saw a newsroom more content on Web clicks and quick-hit journalism than one of quality work based on good sourcing and thorough editing. In 2014, Ann said:

> I just don't think editors demand the same kind of ability. I don't think they monitor what (the reporters) are doing. I just don't see near the level of mentoring and supervision because it's kind of like, "Well,

anything goes. If we can get people to click on it, great." As opposed to what I perceive a generation ago a very kind of methodical, for lack of a better word, approach to how you cover things.

Ann said at her newspaper, Web and social media was a valued commodity, one that influenced news decisions. "Rather than concentrate on producing a compelling product that will be valuable, not only in print but online, I think management decisions have made us focus on 'Gotta get the eyes. Gotta get the clicks,'" she said.

> In all my time I have worked at the (this newspaper) I can never remember somebody killing a story or backing away from a story because it would offend advertising. Yet in the last couple years I've seen that. They are so focused on the bottom line that they can't afford to do anything that's going to hurt that advertising revenue. I suspect that's similar at other papers too because they are so desperate to try to keep sponsors for different things.

Ann feared the standard of quality newspaper journalism was in peril. Hard news focus had been lost, creating what she called an attention deficit disorder kind of news focus. And while she admitted the Internet and other technology had driven the change, management was propagating quick, hit-and-run work. "I think we're in the stage now that as long as we're hanging on to a few veteran reporters who have their own internal standards of quality, we can be a viable product. Once that's gone, it's looking very sad to me for the next generation."

For young journalists, this is an exciting time of great opportunity and change in an industry slow to embrace it. A 30-year-old reporter at a large daily said, "Things are changing and it's an opportunity. Everything changes and we just have to be big girls and boys." For the young, change and adaptation had been slow, and sometimes the previous generation was a hindrance. A 31-year-old photographer explained how he was going to leave his mid-sized newspaper because an older photo chief was impeding his work. Before making a move, the photo chief left the paper. "Before I found out (the photo chief) was leaving, I was going to try to beat him out the door and become a firefighter and do freelance work. Now that he's leaving, there's a bigger opportunity for me to improve and finish the stuff that we were trying to do."

Conclusions

New and different work responsibilities, a diminished workforce, and a clash in cultural norms created persisting stressors for young and veteran journalists alike. Ultimately, not only is the stress compounded, the burnout levels will continue to increase and the migration out of journalism will continue. However, this time the migration will be voluntary, and it will primarily include journalists with less than 10 years in the profession.

For a generation that does not want to work like its parents (prioritize work before family; modest career expectations; lack of work support) (Hershatter and Epstein, 2010; Ng, Schweitzer, and Lyons, 2010), the best and brightest of the younger generation will not remain in newspaper journalism. The traditional newsroom culture, heavy with stress and high work demands, is detrimental to the young journalists and to the journalism produced. In view of this transitional culture, what becomes of journalistic mission and quality of work? What are the new norms permeating the newspaper newsroom and who or what is driving those norms? If the newspaper profession is to survive and thrive, these questions need to be addressed.

In their 35-year retrospective examining burnout research, Schaufeli, Leiter, and Maslach (2009) wrote:

> As for the practice of burnout, it remains to be seen if corporations and public sector organizations are willing to provide the necessary resources to maintain extraordinary efforts from their employees, or whether efforts to inspire extraordinary efforts become a new source of burnout (p. 216).

For newspaper journalists, both appeared to be true. Resources had been depleted, and new and extraordinary work was required – a made-to-order recipe for newsroom burnout. Using up and burning out veteran journalists committed to the profession, and failing to provide guidance to the young people entering it, did not bode well for newspapers, communities, or the culture of journalism.

As financial resources withered, and audiences fractured, newspapers placed the burden of survival on their most valuable resource – their people. But as my research had shown, the unrelenting downward pressure was not sustainable. Burnout would continue to inflict newspaper journalists, possibly creating a new Newsroom Exodus.

References

Aiken, L.H., Clarke, S.P., Sloane, D.M., Sochalski, J., and Silber, J.H. (2002). Hospital nurse staffing and patient mortality, nurse burnout, and job dissatisfaction. *Journal of the American Medical Association*, 288(16): 1987–93.

Brenninkmeijer, V. and Van Yperen, N. (2003), How to conduct research on burnout: Advantages and disadvantages of a unidimensional approach to burnout, *Occupational and Environmental Medicine*, 60(1): 16–21.

Brill, P.L. (1984). The need for an operational definition of burnout. *Family and Community Health*, 6(4), 12–24.

Chappelle, W., McDonald, K., Prince, L., Goodman, T., Ray-Sannerud, B.N., and Thompson, W. (2014). Assessment of occupational burnout in United States Air Force predator/reaper "drone" operators. *Military Psychology*, 26(5–6): 376–85.

Cook, B.B. and Banks, S.R. (1993). Predictors of job burnout in reporters and copy editors. *Journalism Quarterly*, 70(1): 108–17.

Cook, B.B., Banks, S.R., and Turner R.J. (1993) The effects of environment on burnout in the newsroom. *Newspaper Research Journal*, 14(3–4): 123–36.

Craig, D.A. (1999). Influences on editing quality at the *Daily Oklahoman*. *Newspaper Research Journal*, 20(3): 58.

Drew, C. and Philipps, D. (2015). As stress drives off drone operators, Air Force must cut flights. *The New York Times*, June 16.

Dyrbye, L.N., West, C.P., Satele, D., Boone, S., Tan, L., Sloan, J., and Shanafelt, T.D. (2014). Burnout among U.S. medical students, residents, and early career physicians relative to the general U.S. population. *Academic Medicine*, 89(3): 443–51.

Freudenberger, H.J. (1974). Staff burn-out. *Journal of Social Issues*, 30(1), 159–65.

Government Accountability Office (2014). Actions needed to strengthen management of unmanned aerial system pilots. April 10. Located May 6, 2016 from: http://gao .gov/products/GAO-14-316.

Greene, G. (1960). *A burnt-out case*. NY: Viking Press.

Hershatter, A. and Epstein, M. (2010). Millennials and the world of work: An organization and management perspective. *Journal of Business and Psychology*, 25: 211–23.

Krupa, C. (2012). Nearly half of physicians struggle with burnout. *American Medical News*. Located July 1, 2015, from: www.amednews.com/article/20120903/ profession/309039952/2/.

Lazarus, R.S., and Launier, R. (1978). Stress-related transactions between person and environment. In A. Pervis & M. Lewis (Eds.), *Perspectives in Interactional Psychology* (pp. 287–323), New York: Plenum Press.

Martin, D. (1999). Herbert J. Freudenberger, 73, coiner of "burnout," is dead. *The New York Times*, Dec. 5.

Maslach, C. and Jackson, S.E. (1981). The measurement of experienced burnout. *Journal of Occupational Behaviour*, 2(99): 99–113.

Maslach, C. and Jackson, S.E. (1984). Burnout in organizational settings. In Oskamp, S. (Ed.), *Applied Social Psychology Annual* (Vol. 5). Beverly Hills, CA: Sage.

Maslach, C. (1993). Burnout: A multidimensional perspective. In Leiter, W., Maslach, C., and Marek, T. (eds) *Professional Burnout: Recent Developments in Theory and Research*. Washington, D.C.: Taylor & Francis.

Maslach, C., Jackson, S.E., and Leiter, M.P. (1996). *Maslach burnout inventory manual* (3rd ed.). Mountain View, CA: CPP.

Maslach, C., Schaufeli, W.B., and Leiter, M.P. (2001). Job burnout. *Annual Review of Psychology*, 52, 397–422.

Ng, E.S.W., Schweitzer, L., and Lyons, S.T. (2010). New generation, great expectations: A field study of the Millennial Generation. *Journal of Business and Psychology*, 25: 281–92.

Partridge, E. (1950). *A dictionary of slang and unconventional English*, 3rd ed. New York: Macmillan.

Pines, A. M. (1993). Burnout: An existential perspective. In Leiter, W., Maslach, C., and Marek, T. (eds) *Professional burnout: Recent developments in theory and research*. Washington, D.C.: Taylor & Francis.

Richardsen, A. M. and Martinussen, M. (2005). Factorial validity and consistency of the MBI-GS across occupational groups in Norway. *International Journal of Stress Management*, 12(3): 289–97.

Roelofs, J., Verbraak, M., Keijsers, G.P.J., De Bruin, M.B.N., and Schmidt, A.J.M. (2005). Psychometric properties of a Dutch version of the Maslach Burnout Inventory-General Survey (MBI-GS) in individuals with and without clinical burnout. *Stress and Health*, 21: 17–25.

Schaufeli, W., and Enzmann, D. (1998). *The burnout companion to study & practice: A critical analysis*. London: Taylor & Francis.

Schaufeli, W.B., Leiter, M.P., and Maslach, C. (2009). Burnout: 35 years of research and practice. *Career Development International*, 14(3): 204–20.

The American Institute of Stress (2006). Workplace stress. Retrieved July 1, 2015, from: www.stress.org/workplace-stress/.

Webster, T. and Bergman, B. (1999). Occupational stress: Counts and rates. *Compensation and Working Conditions*, Fall: 38–41

3 Feeding the Beast

While in college, John interned at the mid-sized daily newspaper for two summers, catching on as a full-time reporter upon graduation. He was quickly indoctrinated into a cultural expectation of high productivity, overtime work without overtime pay, and an unquestionable allegiance to the newspaper. Although it was a union shop, the ownership group maintained the upper hand. And while ownership did not purposefully abuse the news workers—in fact it treated them rather well—ownership did take advantage of the inherent dedication propagated by journalism's idealism of commitment.

John had always embraced the notion of multimedia journalism. In addition to his newspaper reporting duties he hosted a weekly radio show for more than a decade. When the newspaper began a Web-first initiative, John was an early adopter.

Eventually, after 17 years the work began to take its toll. John was feeling overwhelmed with 12-hour days, 60-hour workweeks and no vacation. His wife was on his case, complaining about work cutting into family time and the lack of pay. "There are days when I work from the minute I get up at 6 o'clock in the morning and my computer's on," he lamented. "I sleep with the phone by my ear in case something happens. (My wife) hates it. We struggle. We struggle badly."

Because John was an early adopter of new technology, management recruited him first to implement their social media initiatives. He said it wasn't a mandate but refusal was not an option, either. "I said, 'I really don't want to wind up doing that. It's going to be extra and more stuff I have to do.' (Management) always used to say, 'It's not going to be more with the blog, Facebook, and Twitter.' I'd always argue, 'Well how can I do the stuff that you want me to do and then all three of those things?' I said, 'Listen guys, I went to (a small college) and it's not a great school, but if I'm not doing it now and I have to do it tomorrow, that's more.'"

Reluctantly, John started a Twitter account in 2012. Within a week he had 1,000 followers that eventually grew to about 8,000. He now has several audiences beyond the newspaper's print edition he felt compelled to satisfy. John said:

> It's strange because you don't know what it is. Do you have (thousands of) followers because you're active or (thousands of) followers because you're good? ... People come to my Twitter to get the information. They don't go to the newspaper's account.

In his newsroom, John is one of the few who have completely embraced the social media movement. However, he said he's trapped in a cycle of his own creation. When asked why he continued to work at his current pace, he said, "What else am I going to do? I enjoy working; I enjoy my job. Would I like a little more money, yeah?

"I've created the mess myself, but if I'm going to do it I want to do it right."

The U.S. Worker

The United States has become the home of the work martyr—workers who take few vacation days, come to work sick, and take pride in being seen at their desks. Recent studies have shown that Americans forego 160 million vacation days a year at a cost of $50 billion—equal to the gross domestic products of Kenya and Guatemala (Oxford Economics, 2014).

In less than a century, the 40-hour workweek was conceived, became the established norm, and became passé. In March 1922, the Ford Motor Company announced it would reduce the workweek from six days to five days, not surpassing 40 hours per week. The move affected more than 50,000 workers as Ford was credited as the one of the first companies to incorporate the 40-hour workweek. At the time, company president Edsel Ford said: "Every man needs more than one day a week for rest and recreation. ... The Ford Company always has sought to promote (an) ideal home life for its employees. We believe that in order to live properly every man should have more time to spend with his family" (*The New York Times*, 1922, p. 1).

It wasn't for unselfish reasons Ford initiated the new policy. A rested worker is more productive, and although employees would work one less day they were expected to produce at the same rate as a six-day workweek. The policy went into affect on May 1, 1926. Soon after, companies throughout the U.S. and the world adopted the Monday through Friday, 40-hour workweek.

Today, the 40-hour workweek in the U.S. is a myth. A 2014 Gallop Poll of full-time workers reported that the average workweek is 47 hours—one hour short of Ford Motor Company's six-day workweek. While 42 percent of the respondents said they work 40-hour weeks, 39 percent worked 50 or more hours. Gallop attributes the increase in hours to personal "gumption," and the number of salaried employees. Hourly employees are restricted from working beyond 40 without overtime pay. The same restriction does not apply to salaried employees. The 2014 Gallop study was not an anomaly. The number of weekly hours worked has remained relatively steady (between 45–47 hours) since 2000 (Saad, 2014).

Studies have shown that excessive work hours are associated with a myriad of ailments such as hypertension (Hayashi, T., Kobayashi, Y., Yamaoka, K., and Yano, E., 1996; Iwasaki et al., 1998), cardiovascular disease (Buell, P. and Breslow, L., 1960; Sokejima, S, and Kagamimori, S., 1998; Liu, Y. and Tanaka, H., 2002), stress (Kirkcaldy, B.D., Trimpop, R., and Cooper, C.L., 1997; Lehmkuhl, L., 1999), chronic infections (Rosenstock et al., 1996) and depression (Glass, J., and Fujimoto, T., 1994; Shields, M., 1999). The studies generally conclude that long hours of work are detrimental to a worker's health, and the ailments that follow can be fatal.

Such was the case for *Pawtucket (R.I.) Evening Times* sports editor Ted Mulcahey. The award-winning journalist was the father of nine who worked for the afternoon newspaper for nearly two decades. Mulcahey would wake at 5 a.m. each day, produce the sports section from 6 a.m. to noon, return home until about 6:30 p.m. and then cover an evening sporting event. He'd return home at about 1 a.m., sleep for four hours and start anew in the morning (Mulcahey v. New England Newspapers, Inc., 1985).

Prior to his death on Oct. 13, 1978, Mulcahey was taking medication for diabetes and high blood pressure. Five days earlier after covering a Philadelphia Eagles vs. New England Patriots NFL game, he had suffered a cerebral hemorrhage. Mulcahey's wife, Helen, filed a worker's compensation lawsuit claiming the stress and workload of Ted's job contributed to his death.

In Mulcahey v. New England Newspapers, Inc. (1985), a certified cardiologist who examined Mulcahey upon his arrival at Pawtucket Memorial Hospital testified that meeting numerous deadlines "probably aggravated" Mulcahey's hypertension and diabetes, ultimately contributing to his death. The Mulcahey family physician told the court, "The circumstances at the game caused his death, the workload, I'd say it's the probable cause of death." The physician also said Mulcahey's stressful employment aggravated his hypertension and diabetes (Mulcahey v. New England Newspapers, Inc., 1985).

The Rhode Island Supreme Court agreed and awarded Helen Mulcahey $55,000 in retroactive benefits, plus about $185 per week for the rest of her life (Mulcahey v. New England Newspapers, Inc., 1985). Helen Mulcahey collected the benefit until the time of her death on April 21, 2015, at the age of 95 (*Pawtucket Times*, 2015).

Speaking from her home in Lincoln, Rhode Island, Mulcahey's daughter, Liz, said her father never complained about his work. "Although it was a lot of hours he got a lot of enjoyment out of it. It wasn't a drag on him. It was just a lot of hours and a lot of deadlines to meet" (Liz Mulcahey interview, 2013).

Workload Stress

The American Institute of Stress lists a variety of reasons for workplace stress, but "workload" tops the list at 46 percent. That trumps "people issues" (28 percent), "juggling work/personal lives" (20 percent), and "lack of job security" (6 percent). An increase in stressors—workload, for example—increases stress and the ailments that can follow (The American Institute of Stress, 2006).

The National Institute for Occupational Safety examined data from three independent studies and concluded that 40 percent of workers reported their jobs as "very or extremely stressful" (National Institute for Occupational Safety and Health, 1999, p. 4). In its study, NIOSH defined stress as "the harmful physical and emotional responses that occur when the requirements of the job do not match the capabilities, resources, or needs of the worker" (p. 6).

Additionally, workplace stress sufferers miss on average 23 workdays a year (Webster and Bergman, 1999; Health and Safety Executive, 2015). The expenditures associated with stress-related accidents, absenteeism, turnover, reduced productivity, medical and insurance costs, and workers' compensation costs U.S. businesses about $300 billion each year (American Health Institute, 2006).

Workload stress for newspaper journalists is nothing new. Deadlines have always dictated workflow; editorial page newshole requires filling; and news happens. Coping with stressors is an individual proposition. As some journalists thrive under stressful conditions, others do not fare as well. Experiences—time on the job and different kinds of work experiences—allow for journalists to adapt in stressful situations. Theoretically, when producing the newspaper, experienced journalists can better cope with unexpected occurrences than younger journalists. If a story or photograph falls through, a computer crashes, or breaking news happens on deadline, the more experienced journalists have traditionally directed a workable solution. Veterans were equipped and expected to solve unexpected problems.

Generally, work experiences allow workers to build a reservoir of coping resources. When new work habits are introduced, and a work culture is changing, the internal resources for veteran workers to cope with stressful situations are diminished. When stressors accumulate, workers tap into the reservoir to minimize stress. During times of unique change, the veteran employee no longer has a pool of experiences to draw upon, which further compounds stress. For example, in 2011 while covering an NBA game between the Houston Rockets and Minnesota Timberwolves an Associated Press reporter sent a tweet after a referee made what appeared to be a bad call. The tweet was sent after the reporter overheard a discussion between the referee and Minnesota Coach Kurt Rambis. The tweet read: "Ref Bill Spooner told Rambis he'd 'get it back' after a bad call. Then he made an even worse call on Rockets. That's NBA officiating folks" (Associated Press, 2011).

The referee, Bill Spooner, filed a defamation lawsuit against the Associated Press and the AP reporter, Jon Krawczynski. Spooner said the tweet led to an NBA disciplinary investigation. He also said his professional reputation was damaged. Spooner was asking for more than $75,000 in damages, and that Krawczynski remove the tweet from his account (Associated Press, 2011).

The Associated Press implemented a strict Facebook and Twitter policy in 2009. In part, the Twitter policy read: "We're still the AP. Don't report things or break news that we haven't published, no matter the format, and that includes retweeting unconfirmed information not fit for AP's wires" (Socialmedia.biz, 2009). Although a policy was in place at the time of Krawczynski's tweet, it was incomplete. The policy did not necessarily address hearsay, which in this case Krawczynski had tweeted part of a conversation he overheard between a referee and a coach. As an editor who encouraged live coverage through social media, what was the protocol for addressing the controversy between the reporter and referee?

Traditional journalistic practice would suggest unconfirmed information – hearsay—should be vetted before publication. But in an immediate-information world, time for vetting is compromised. Tweets are seldom edited before distribution. The editor had no previous experience in rectifying the immediacy of posting information on social media with timely vetting of the information. The editor did not have a reservoir of resources of experiences to draw upon.

The case was settled out of court as the AP agreed to pay $20,000 for Spooner's litigation costs, and remove the tweet (Associated Press, 2011). The sides also mutually agreed to this statement:

AP and its reporter Jon Krawczynski learned through discovery that referee Bill Spooner and coach Kurt Rambis have both consistently and independently denied that Mr. Spooner told the coach "he'd get it back" in an exchange that occurred after a disputed call against the Timberwolves on Jan. 24, 2011, as Mr. Krawczynski had tweeted from courtside that night. Mr. Spooner has testified that he instead told the coach he would "get back" to him after reviewing videotape of the play during a halftime break.

The NBA promptly investigated at the time and concluded that Mr. Spooner had acted properly. AP was initially unaware of the investigation and does not contest the NBA's finding. During the game, Mr. Krawczynski tweeted what he believed he had heard. Mr. Krawczynski acknowledges the possibility that he misunderstood what Mr. Spooner said and has therefore removed the Tweet from his APKrawczynski Twitter feed (Associated Press, 2011).

The Associated Press revised its social media policy in 2013. Although the revised policy does not address hearsay in original tweets, it does include this paragraph about retweets: "Staffers should steer clear of retweeting rumors and hearsay. They can, however, feel free to reply to such tweets in order to seek further information, as long as they're careful to avoid repeating the questionable reports" (Associated Press, 2013).

In the new information age, unforeseen stressors force newspaper newsrooms to adapt as incidents occur. Increased workload, and new and different work, has complicated challenges for news workers.

Among CareerCast.com's most stressful jobs of 2016, journalists were listed twice in the Top 10 – No. 8: Broadcaster, and No. 9: Newspaper Reporter (CareerCast.com, 2016). For several years, "newspaper reporter" has been among CareerCast.com's Top 10 most stressful jobs list, citing a low annual median salary ($37,200 in 2016) and a growth outlook of minus-9 in 2016. Interestingly, in my 2009 and 2014 research, career regret remained relatively unchanged. When asked, "If you could go back and choose a different career, would you?" among the 3,400 respondents 33 percent said they would not go into newspaper journalism.

Role Overload

At 41, Chris had been working at his daily newspaper for 14 years. During that time, he filled many roles, but when we talked in 2014 he was carrying three titles, including assistant news editor.

Chris' newspaper had gone through two ownership changes and several rounds of layoffs in the previous decade. The newsroom has been reduced by more than 50 percent, leaving rows of empty desks that had yet to be removed. He described morale as "up and down," and said many of his colleagues did not feel valued. "At this point, if you're still here, you're here because you love it or there's a reason behind it," he said. "The people who are here are good enough that we try to put our heads down and push through the crap."

Pushing through the crap included absorbing additional responsibilities, adapting to new online work demands, and working longer hours. Veteran news workers were shifted into unfamiliar roles as the newspaper expanded its online initiatives. "They've taken people who were really good at something and made them do the Web, and they absolutely, positively hate it but they have to do it," Chris said. "I think because of that the overall quality suffers."

Because of the reduced workforce, news decisions became more complicated. Chris said the newspaper had to be more selective in its coverage.

> As a whole we have to weigh what our community wants and we have to take an educated guess. We're deciding what people want to read. But if our job is to inform the readers and we're not given the space and the resources, we're not doing it as well as we used to. Is there less news than there was 10 years ago or so? I think we know that's not true. There's just as much so something is being left out every day.

Chris started searching for a new job, and actually, a new career. His frustration with the workload, pace, and lack of job security has taken its toll. "I'll never work for another newspaper," he said. "I don't apply a lot but when I do I mean it and want it. My problem is there is just not another field out there that I like as much as journalism."

Chris' frustrations are not unfamiliar to long-time working newspaper journalists. In more than a decade of researching newsrooms and news workers, role overload has been a primary contributor to burnout and job dissatisfaction. In fact, role overload rated highest among those in Chris' newsroom in 2014 compared to a national sample of more than 1,600 respondents. Chris' colleagues also had the highest rate of burnout and lowest rate of satisfaction compared with the national group.

By definition, role overload examines the basic principle of work demands surpassing the time to complete the work. The workload measurement weighs how well workers are able to complete the assigned tasks in the allotted time. Developers of the measurement wrote, in part that role overload was: "… (i.e., the conflict between time and organizational demands concerning the quantity of work to be done)" (Bacharach, Bamberger, and Conley, 1990, p. 202).

In my research with journalists, role overload from 2007 to 2014 increased at a statistically significant level, as did the rate of burnout. To get to the core issues involving job demands, 2009 and 2014 survey respondents were asked, "Since starting in your newsroom, do you work differently?" Among the nearly 2,000 respondents in the 2009 study, 68 percent responded "yes." By 2014, the number had jumped to 83 percent.

To delve deeper into the issue, respondents were asked, "If you do work differently, how so?" In 2009, of the 1,250 journalists in the study 68 percent said job demands—more work, less time to conduct the work, working faster, taking on multiple tasks and job titles–were the primary work issues. Job demand issues for men (72 percent) were of greater concern than for women (63 percent) in the study. Two additional issues concerning work effort included quality of work, and working in a culture of fear. Twenty-one percent of journalists said diminished quality was a result of the new work demands. As for the culture of fear, overall 8 percent said it was an issue. However, 11 percent of women and only 6 percent of men mentioned fear in the open-ended responses. Representing many respondents working in a culture of fear, a 40-year-old female photographer at a mid-sized (between 50,001–100,000 circulation) newspaper wrote:

> I find I am trying to keep one step ahead of my coworkers. We used to be more like a family of loving siblings now it seems like we are looking at each other wondering who is next on the chopping block.

Others discussed being "expendable," volunteering for bad assignments to appease management, and keeping their heads down so they were not noticed. Interestingly, in 2009 online and social media objectives were not an issue. When asked about working differently, less than 1 percent mentioned online or social media. At that time, newsrooms were adjusting to the reduced workforce and committed to staying the course. New online initiatives were not ignored but they were not a priority. Instead, newsrooms were realigning work responsibilities to meet reasonable work expectations.

Also in 2009, data indicated there was a brewing contempt for management. A 44-year-old, male reporter at a large newspaper (more than 100,001 circulation) said: "I am more hesitant to question editors directly, because I feel they laid off complainers. We all do more, and are paid less, and managers have not once acknowledged this fact. That makes me very unhappy and cynical."

A 55-year-old male, page designer said:

> The job now has different demands than in the past. Emphasis is more on meeting stringent deadlines than actual content (which runs contrary to what I believe journalism should be). No one cares about content, why should I? And the powers that be don't care anymore that I don't care, and that's the saddest part of all.

By 2014, the newsroom tone had shifted. While job demands still dominated the "work differently" conversation, it had adopted a more expansive meaning. Working harder and faster still persisted, however, Web and social media initiatives were the primary causes of work demands. For 69 percent of the nearly 1,000 comments from journalists, Web and social media were responsible for the additional workload. Not unexpectedly, online responsibilities became more burdensome for the older generation of journalists than the under-30 crowd. For journalists under 30, only 15 percent mentioned online, social media, or digital work. For those 31 to 60, the online and social media workload was included in 75 percent of the comments. The differences between the young newsroom workers and the more experienced can be summed up by a 27-year-old male sports editor at a small newspaper (under 50,000 circulation): "FYI: I've only been a journalist for two years, so the changes newspapers have gone through in the last 15 years haven't been part of my reality."

For the older journalists, the reality was far different. A 33-year-old male copy editor who had been at the same small newspaper for 11 years said, "Less time spent reading stories, coming up with creative designs. Time now spent posting to website, rearranging stories on the Web, updating Twitter and Facebook, focusing more on making earlier deadlines than quality work." A 43-year-old female reporter at a large newspaper said, "My workload has increased from having to do breaking online postings in addition to overnight and project pieces. More journalists are shooting their own photos and video and are responsible for coming up with more graphic packages."

Progressively, online and social media became more of a work demand issue for older journalists. For the 51–60 age group, 78 percent said the Internet was the cause of their increased work demands. And many were not happy about it. Summarizing the feelings of many, a 56-year-old male reporter with 17 years at his current newspaper said:

> Collectively, we are forced to produce more and encouraged to research less. We have less time, more foolish requirements to meet - Twitter and Facebook quotas, digital "shoveling," iPhone photo galleries – and far less opportunity or encouragement to do big-picture, comprehensive, and groundbreaking reporting. We spend far more time on cheap-thrill police news, salacious clickbait, and dopey space-fillers. And about 75 percent of our news staff is gone since the early 2000s.

Other issues mentioned in the "work differently" responses included quality of work issues (15 percent) and changes in jobs because of departures (11 percent). In the 2009 study, job changes for those under 30 were mentioned in less than 1 percent of the responses. For journalists under 30,

18 percent in 2014 said they had been promoted or changed jobs. There was a clear shift in managerial opportunities for younger staff members. The creation of online and social media editor positions, in concert with mass departures, allowed young journalists to climb the career ladder much quicker than previous generations.

Quality of work concerns among women remained constant throughout the age groups at about 20 percent. For men, 13 percent of the respondents bemoaned the sacrifice of quality for quantity but the numbers are skewed. For those 50 and younger, 19 percent mentioned quality as an issue. For the over-51 crowd, only 8 percent discussed quality. One consideration for the skew could have been that older journalists in management positions continued to tout the newspaper's high quality contrary to their staff's perspective. In the 2014 study, 33 percent of those 51–60 were managers—the highest among the age groups by nearly 10 percentage points.

During interviews with nearly 100 journalists in 2014, workload demands were a prominent issue. At 42, Charles had been a reporter for his small newspaper for 13 years. Because of layoffs and attrition, he was considered the senior reporter on a staff surrounded by many new hires in their 20s. Charles was an old-school reporter, beating the street for stories and conducting face-to-face interviews. He was a trusted voice in the community, particularly with his coverage of local business and government issues. By his estimate, Charles produced about 600 articles a year. But even as a high producer, the new work demands were taking a toll.

> The workload is significant and it's increased. That's been a definite productivity squeeze that's happened here and across the industry. Because of the challenge to monetize the business to the levels it's been in the past, that's been the response from management – to squeeze productivity. That certainly has happened with the news staff.

Charles admitted his reporting had changed with the additional work demands and adaptation of online work. He said he produced more one-source stories, a taboo practice in the past but now more readily accepted.

> The easiest thing to do when you have to write that many stories is to not make the extra phone call. You have to move on and keep the beast fed. ... Whereas before it was, "I feel good about that but I bet you so-and-so could tell me something that would add additional perspective." You'd make that call 10 years ago. Today you don't make that call.

Although Charles' newspaper incentivized clicks, he said he didn't chase them. He said he was proud of his work and how he approached the job.

Charles had greater concerns for the younger staff members at his newspaper who haven't had the experience or training. And, he admitted, he didn't have time to indoctrinate the younger journalists to the established newsroom norms where one-source stories were not ideal.

It's more challenging for a younger reporter. Here's the thing, are the younger reporters even thinking in that mindset (of one-source stories)? They weren't here doing it 10 years ago the way we did it so it may never even come to their minds that you can do it a different way.

Conclusions

For many, journalism is not just a job or career, but a calling deeply entwined with self-identity. Amid the tsunami of staff cuts and expanded work expectations, management's reliance upon their workers' noble commitment has kept the trains on schedule. Now burdened with more responsibilities, different types of work, and a diminished workforce, newsroom survivors are encumbered with unrelenting and sometimes unmanageable workloads.

Newsrooms have always worked under the crush of deadline and the daily delivery. The day-to-day requirements mandate that the news bag be stuffed with local, state, regional, national, and international news. Sports pages brim with Little League scores to full-blown Major League box scores. Entertainment, Business, and Features sections fill out the bundle. Each day it takes a small army to assemble the "morning miracle."

But now, fulfilling the daily promise isn't good enough. The media-fractured audience wants more: more news, more information, more fun stuff to fill their idle minds. They want engagement and entertainment and to be heard. They want to promote and support those in agreement and berate those who disagree. Newspaper journalists no longer simply navigate toward the midnight deadline; they traverse into an information world sculpted by boundless deadlines and perpetual demands. And the toll has been mighty.

In part, assembly-line journalism fulfills the audience demands, but it is unfulfilling to the newsroom producer. Half-sized staffs are designated to time-and-a-half workloads. After journalists left or were asked to leave newsrooms, others were "promoted" with two and sometimes three new titles. Beats were bundled and given to reporters who were already overwhelmed. Copy editors were customizing and shoveling content to blogs and Facebook and Twitter. News editors faced the challenge of appropriately distributing the information to meet audience demands. Photographers were learning video techniques as graphic artists created interactive presentations. The pace became unbearable and unfulfilling. As a 25-year veteran put it: "Everyone is the proverbial gerbil on the wheel."

Traditionally, through years of work and a plethora of experiences veteran journalists had the resources to guide the staff through stressful times. However, the new, unfamiliar work left many veterans ill-equipped to provide that guidance. Newsroom norms and expectations were in flux, allowing for the younger generation to shape the future of newspaper journalism – or at least how it is practiced. What isn't known is what that future holds in terms of journalistic practices. What is known is that unless there is a reconfiguration of workload demands, the news worker will continue to bear the brunt of unyielding stress.

Newspaper news workers remain committed to feeding a news beast that is bigger and more demanding than ever. Motivated by obligation or fear, journalists navigated through staff reductions that pressed them to work harder and faster. Soon after, they were then asked to adopt online, multimedia, and social media responsibilities. Although news workers complied, the downward pressure to please all audiences all the time has taken its toll. And the human labor costs in terms of burnout, job satisfaction, and work quality are evident.

References

Associated Press (2013). Social media guidelines for AP employees. May. www.ap.org/Images/Social-Media-Guidelines_tcm28-9832.pdf.

Associated Press (2011). NBA, AP reach settlement in lawsuit over reporter's tweet, Dec. 7. www.nba.com/2011/news/12/07/nba-twitter-lawsuit-settlement.ap/index.html.

Bacharach, S.B., Bamberger, P., and Conley, S.C. (1990). Work processes, role conflict, and role overload: The case of nurses and engineers in the public sector. *Work and Occupation*, 17(2), 199–228.

Buell, P. and Breslow, L. (1960). Mortality from coronary heart disease in Californian men who work long hours. *Journal of Chronic Diseases*. (11):615–26.

CareerCast.com (2016). The most stressful jobs of 2016. January 7. www.careercast.com/jobs-rated/most-stressful-jobs-2016.

Glass, J. and Fujimoto, T. (1994). Housework, paid work, and depression among husbands and wives. *Journal of Health and Social Behavior*. 35(2):179–91.

Hayashi, T., Kobayashi, Y., Yamaoka, K., and Yano, E. (1996). Effect of overtime work on 24-hour ambulatory blood pressure. *Journal of Occupational and Environmental Medicine*. 38: 1007–11.

Health and Safety Executive (2015). Working days lost. October. www.hse.gov.uk/statistics/dayslost.htm.

Iwasaki, K., Sasaki, T., Oka, T., and Hisanaga, N. (1998). Effect of working hours on biological functions related to cardiovascular system among salesmen in a machinery manufacturing company. *Industrial Health*. 36(4): 361–7.

Kirkcaldy, B.D., Trimpop, R., and Cooper, C.L. (1997). Working hours, job stress, work satisfaction, and accident rates among medical practitioners, consultants, and allied personnel. *International Journal of Stress Management*. 4: 79–87.

Lehmkuhl, L. (1999). Health effects of long work hours. "32 Hours" Organization Report. www.wen.net/32hours/Health%20Effects%20v2.htm.

Liu, Y. and Tanaka, H. (2002). The Fukuoka Heart Study Group. Overtime work, insufficient sleep, and risk of non-fatal acute myocardial infarction in Japanese men. *Occupational and Environmental Medicine.* 59: 447–51.

Mulcahey, L. (2013). Interview with subject. July 25.

National Institute for Occupational Safety and Health (1999). Stress at work. Center for Disease Control. http://www.cdc.gov/niosh/docs/99-101/.

Oxford Economics (2014). All work and no pay: The impact of forfeited time. *Project: Time Off.* October. www.projecttimeoff.com/research/all-work-and-no-pay-impact-forfeited-time

Pawtucket Times (2015). Helen F. (Duffy) Mulcahey. Obituary. April 22. www.legacy.com/obituaries/pawtuckettimes/obituary.aspx?pid=174687535.

Rosenstock, S.J., Andersen, L.P., Rosenstock, C.V., Bonnevie, O., and Jorgensen, T. (1996). Socioeconomic factors in Helicobacter pylori infection among Danish adults. *American Journal of Public Health*, 86(11): 1539–44.

Saad, L. (2014). The "40-hour" workweek is actually longer–by seven hours. Gallup. August 29. www.gallup.com/poll/175286/hour-workweek-actually-longer-seven-hours.aspx.

Shields, M. (1999). Long working hours and health. *Health Rep.* 11(2):33–48.

Socialmedia.biz (2009). Associated Press's social media policy. June 23. http://socialmedia.biz/social-media-policies/associated-presss-social-media-policy/.

Sokejima, S and Kagamimori, S. (1998). Working hours as a risk factor for acute myocardial infarction in Japan: Case-control study. *BMJ.* June: 317; 775–80.

The New York Times (1922). 5-day, 40-hour week for Ford employees; New permanent working policy with Saturday and Sunday shut-down, is announced. Retain $6 a day minimum change affecting 50,000 men will mean 3,000 increase in force, Edsel Ford says. March 25, p. 1. http://query.nytimes.com/gst/abstract.html?res=9 80CE3DD1639EF3ABC4D51DFB5668389639EDE

The American Institute of Stress (2006). Workplace stress. www.stress.org/workplace-stress/

Webster, T., and Bergman, B. (1999). Occupational stress: Counts and rates. *Compensation and Working Conditions.* Fall: 38–41.

4 Job Satisfaction

Kelly expected to be a newspaper lifer. Growing up in a family of journalists, newspapering was a natural fit. Four years after graduating from a Top 10 journalism program, Kelly was a 26-year-old copy editor working at a 125,000-daily circulation newspaper. Similar to so many newspapers at the time, layoffs and departures were common in 2008. At Kelly's newspaper, she said when a full-time staff member left the newsroom, he or she was replaced with a part-time, less skilled worker. During that time, the burden of work responsibility heightened for the newsroom mainstays. "If you're a stronger, better worker, the way our system is set up, you end up doing more work," Kelly said in 2008. "You kind of punish yourself for being faster and better. And that's one thing management just seems to accept and looks the other way."

In tandem with staff cuts, Kelly's newspaper was initiating a vague Web-first policy without providing much guidance. "Basically their philosophy seems to be as many news updates on the Web as possible, which means that we're publishing content that would be going into tomorrow's paper on the Web the night before," she said. "It gets a little sticky, in my opinion, of whether that's really worthwhile."

The tumultuous transitions in her early work life had Kelly re-examining her career choice. She admitted her level of job satisfaction was in a state of flux, and despite her love of journalism, she said her newspaper future was uncertain.

> I feel I've entered the business on its downswing and it makes me sad. I really care what newspapers stand for. Our problem is we still pay lip service to caring about what we used to care about when we look the other way and cut jobs and cut the budget. I'm concerned that I'm not going to have a career in this business, and frankly I've been thinking about what I'll do next, which I have mixed feelings about. I come from a newspaper family and it would be hard to imagine not working for a newspaper because that's what I've always done.

Since the mid-1900s, researchers have been examining job satisfaction levels of newspaper journalists. Although pinpointing determinants of job satisfaction is a difficult proposition, researchers have been able to establish patterns of satisfaction and causes of that satisfaction.

Granted, anyone who has heard a newspaper journalist gripe about his editor, his colleagues, his work assignments, or his unappreciated status in the newsroom would quickly realize "satisfaction" and "newspaper job" rarely co-exist in comfort. Perhaps legendary *New York Tribune* editor and one-time presidential candidate Horace Greeley stated it properly: "Journalism will kill you, but it will keep you alive while you're at it" (Andrews, 1990).

Finding Satisfaction

The newspaper industry is not the first to undergo a seismic industrial transformation. Since the industrial revolution, cost cutting, new technologies, massive layoffs, restructuring, and wayward managerial initiatives have created discontent and dissatisfaction among the workforce.

A prime example is what occurred at the Fremont, California, General Motors plant in the late 1970s and early 1980s. By 1979, even the United Auto Workers (UAW) union representing Fremont plant employees labeled them the worst workforce in the automobile industry (Langfitt, 2010). Management belittled employees, treated suggestions as defiance, and restricted the use of office restrooms (Clark, 1993). The workers suffered high rates of alcoholism and drug abuse, skipped an average of one workday a week, organized wildcat strikes, and had a terrible record of producing poor quality cars (Oldsmobile Cutless) and quantity (24 hours to produce a car compared with about 16 hours in a Toyota Japanese plant) (Clark, 1993; Pfeffer, 1998). Workers would drink on the job, routinely have sex in the plant, and to get back at their managers, deliberately sabotage vehicles by placing Coke bottles inside door panels to annoy customers with the constant rattling (Langfitt, 2010).

A series of layoffs at the Fremont plant began in 1979 and continued for the next couple years. Finally, in 1982 GM shuttered the plant, putting 5,800 workers out of work (Schore, 1984). In the months that followed, there were numerous reports of heart attacks and divorces. Eight former employees committed suicide within six months of the closure (Schore, 1984).

What happened next is automotive legend. Toyota officials wanted to gain experience with U.S. workers and suppliers. GM officials were interested in learning the successful Toyota Production System (TPS). The two companies formulated a joint venture, New United Motor Manufacturing, Inc. (NUMMI). In 1985, hiring back 85 percent of the previous Fremont plant employees, NUMMI started manufacturing Chevy Novas. With the same union in the same plant using many of the same workers, NUMMI succeeded where GM failed. The change in production system and management practices was the difference (Pfeffer, 1998). Workers were given job security and training. Managers incorporated about 80 percent of workers' suggestions, allowing employees to design their own work stations. Employees were valued and felt invested in the company. In just a few years, the Fremont plant was considered one of the most efficient and welcoming in the U.S. (Clark, 1993). Production was up (16 hours to assemble a car) and defects were cut in half (Pfeffer, 1998). In discussing the Fremont turnaround, GM Representative Joel Smith told NPR in 2010:

> For too long, the American worker has been maligned, criticized, called bad names for building lousy cars. And Mr. Toyota, if you would please deliver this challenge to our friends in Japan, we intend to build the best quality car in the world. Thank you (Langfitt, 2010).

The Fremont NUMMI plant continued to produce high-quality vehicles until 2010 when it would close for good, laying off 4,700 workers. GM had filed for bankruptcy in 2009, and shortly after pulled out of the joint venture with Toyota. On the heels of its worst reported annual losses in the company's history, Toyota officials said the Fremont plant was no longer economically viable. So, on April 1, 2010, the final car rolled off the Fremont assembly line—a Toyota Corolla (Zimmerman and Dolan, 2009; Langfitt, 2010).

The successful transformation of the Fremont plant can be attributed to workers' job satisfaction and management's understanding that a happy worker is a good worker. Although elements of job satisfaction might vary between individuals, satisfaction on the job is defined by the relationship a person has with his or her work. A worker cannot expect the work environment to fulfill his or her complete emotional wants and needs. Equally, the employer cannot expect that the standardization of work to be completely fulfilling to the worker. In his seminal research examining hundreds of studies, Edwin Locke (1976) wrote:

> … job satisfaction may be viewed as the pleasurable emotional state resulting from the perception of one's job as fulfilling or allowing the fulfillment of one's important job values, providing these values are compatible with one's needs. (Values refer to what one considers beneficial, whereas needs are the conditions actually required for one's well-being) (p. 1342).

Work satisfaction is contingent on internal and external factors. People work for money, to earn a title and be a boss, or for social status—all external factors. People also work for personal achievement, to learn new things, to be socially engaged, and to do something meaningful—all internal factors. In his book, *Why We Work*, Swarthmore College Psychology Professor Barry Schwartz (2015) addresses the notions of work and why we do it. He wrote:

> The opportunity to do our work "right," to do our best, to be encouraged to develop and learn, to feel appreciated by coworkers and supervisors, to feel that our opinions count, to feel that what we do is important, and to have good friends at work are all aspects of work (p. 3).

Early in its history, Apple Computer was designed to fulfill workers' internal and external needs. Founded by Stephen Wozniak and Steve Jobs in 1976, Apple's unique culture included a separate building for the Macintosh design team that featured a pirate flag flying over it. The cult-like ideology that they were changing the world by developing a home computer for every man was a recruiting call for the best and brightest employees. In the 1993 Apple Employee Handbook, the company outlined its values for individual performance:

> We expect individual commitment and performance above the standard for our industry. Only thus will we make the profits that permit us to seek our other corporate objectives. Each employee can and must make a difference. In the final analysis, individuals determine the character and strength of Apple (Apple Employee Handbook, 1993).

The handbook outlined cultural traditions such as open communication with management, celebrating important life events of employees, acknowledging individual achievements within the teamwork structure, and bagel and cream cheese Fridays (Pfeffer, 1998). Apple was a company that recognized workers as an important asset to be respected and cherished. But when sales dipped, Apple implemented a series of job cuts—20 percent in 1985; 10 percent in 1991; 14 percent in 1993; 33 percent in 1997 (Pfeffer, 1998). The layoffs chipped away at Apple's culture of trust and appreciation, particularly in how the cuts occurred. The uncertainty created a culture of fear, pushing the best people to leave. On days when layoffs occurred, workers were called into the managers' offices and informed of their dismissal, escorted to their desks to gather personal items, and then escorted by security to the door (Pfeffer, 1998).

The culture of support and open communication was shattered among the remaining employees.

In his book, *The Human Equation*, Jeffrey Pfeffer examined how the negative cultural shift occurred and what it meant for Apple. To boost profits, a company cut costs by reducing the workforce. What followed were cuts in salary and training, part-time workers replacing full-time, and promotions and hiring freezes. "These measures logically and inevitably reduce motivation, satisfaction, loyalty to the company and intentions to remain with it, and focus on the job (as contrasted with discussing rumors and sharing complaints with coworkers)" (Pfeffer, 1998, p. 26). Pfeffer labeled it the "Downward Performance Spiral – Performance Problems" (low profits, high costs, and poor customer service) led to an "Organizational Response" (layoffs, wage freeze, hiring freeze, and more part-time hires), which led to "Individual Behaviors" (decreased motivation and effort, increased turnover, and reduced job satisfaction) (Pfeffer, 1998).

Losing Satisfaction

Shane was a 38-year-old copy editor and page designer at a mid-sized newspaper. He had been with the company for nine years. Since his time at the paper, Shane said job cuts and a reduced newshole made it difficult for the staff to reach the same level of work as it had in the past. "It's a lot more hectic pace than it used to be," he said. "It used to be you had plenty of time to concentrate on your work. Now, quality and speed have come together, and there's probably a few more errors."

But Shane wasn't a complainer. In fact, he was thrilled he still had a job. Shane's newsroom had a strong Guild, and similar to many unions, when cuts were needed they came from the bottom. During a series of layoffs between 2008 and 2010, Shane was among the bottom five with the least seniority. He was laid off on two occasions when the bottom five were cut.

"When you're at the bottom of that seniority list in the union you have that hanging over your head," he said. "It's kind of like being on death row. The next round of cuts might be coming for you. There is a bit of anxiety around here about job security."

During his first layoff, Shane received a reprieve when another staffer came forward and volunteered to be laid off. His job was safe, but only temporarily. About a year later, more cuts came. Again, Shane was on the chopping block. Many times he had witnessed security escorting his friends from the building after being handed pink slips. The second time Shane was laid off, he was offered a bonus to stay for 30 days during a transition period. He met with human relations to have the "what's next" conversation. "I was very much hurt when that happened," he said of the second layoff. "I know it's a numbers thing and you're just at a certain point on the seniority list, but you still feel hurt because you feel you've done a pretty good job and you're valuable. But that's not taken into consideration."

Again, Shane received a reprieve when another staffer came forward to accept a severance package. However, he admitted, after being laid off twice and feeling devalued, the level of trust was gone. "There's not an air of that in the newsroom. Just everybody was here when the axe was dropping regularly. When it happens to that degree of frequency I'm not sure you ever quite regain the trust."

Four years later, Shane was still at the newspaper. Others had left for better jobs or a better life. The newspaper rebounded a bit, even making a few new hires. With each hire, Shane gained a little more job security as he moved up the seniority list. Last he checked, there were at least five other colleagues who would lose their jobs before him.

Among a sample of nearly 1,700 respondents in my 2014 study, journalists in Shane's newsroom reported the lowest level of job satisfaction. Shane said his level of job satisfaction varied through the years, some of it driven by fear of being laid off, but much of it influenced by personal pride and satisfaction in his work.

For journalists, job satisfaction has always seemed to be influenced by the highs and lows of the job. In 1935 following the suicide of a foreign correspondent, an editorial in *The Guild Reporter* summarized the adrenaline peaks and valleys of journalism. In part, the editorial said that while reporters "share the exciting adventures and power of the people they write about, their spirits are high. But when the shot in the arm ends, too often they have no other resources or satisfactions left and life seems unbearably flat" (Lee, 1937, p. 603).

Dating to the 1960s, the dimension of job satisfaction among journalists evolved beyond the simple thrill of chasing a good story. One of the earliest studies conducted by Merrill Samuelson (1962) discovered that one-third of journalism graduates left their newspaper careers because they were less satisfied than those who stayed. Personal duties, poor leadership, and little expectation to advance in the profession were among the reasons satisfaction waned for those who departed (Samuelson, 1962).

The lineage of journalism job satisfaction studies continued in 1971 when Johnstone, Slawski, and Bowman surveyed more than 1,300 newspaper workers and learned that journalistic standards played a primary role in satisfaction, and between 20 and 25 percent of young journalists questioned their professional commitment. Johnstone et al., (1976) wrote: "Dissatisfaction within this group does not seem to stem from economic opportunities, but job dissatisfaction for many young newsmen has to do more with professional considerations—discrepancies between journalistic ideals and day-to-day practices" (p. 154). However, journalists' commitment to the profession remained steadfast—83 percent said they expected to remain in news work for at least the next five years.

No group of journalism researchers has examined journalists' job satisfaction more than the one led by David Weaver and G. Cleveland Wilhoit. Spanning decades dating to the early 1980s, Weaver and Wilhoit produced annual reports on the state of journalism and journalists, including the notion of work satisfaction. Beginning with the 1971 research of Johnstone et al., Weaver and Wilhoit recorded a continuous decline in newspaper news workers' job satisfaction through the 1990s (Weaver and Wilhoit, 1986; Weaver and Wilhoit, 1996). In their 1971 study, Johnstone et al., reported that about 49 percent of journalists said they were "very satisfied" with their work. By 1992, Weaver and Wilhoit (1996) found that only 27 percent said they were "very satisfied." Weaver and Wilhoit (1996) wrote:

> Journalists in 1992 appeared to want to lead normal lives. They were less willing to suffer the dislocation and unpredictable schedules that were accepted by an earlier generation, especially in a competitive environment in which newsrooms were expected to do much more with fewer resources, and where there was little hope of professional advancement in an era of stalled growth (p. 118–119).

By 2002, Weaver, Beam, Brownless, Voakes, and Wilhoit, (2007) found a slight increase in job satisfaction from the previous work, with 33 percent saying they were "very satisfied." Not surprisingly, during the turbulent transformation in the newsrooms that followed, the trend did not hold. In 2013, Weaver and Willnat (2014) reported that those "very satisfied" in their work had dipped to an all-time low of 23 percent. Also, more journalists said they had less autonomy in their work and felt journalism was headed in the wrong direction. Weaver and Willnat wrote (2013):

> When asked about the "most important problem facing journalism today," the journalists in our study mentioned the following issues most often: declining profits (mentioned by 20.4 percent); threats to profession from online media (11.4 percent); job cuts and downsizing (11.3 percent); the need for a new business model and funding structure (10.8 percent); hasty reporting (9.9 percent) (p. 3).

Throughout the decades of research, a few issues have remained core determinants of job satisfaction among newspaper journalists, including autonomy of work, the editorial mission to serve the community, and producing quality work. The number of journalists intending to leave the profession has remained relatively constant throughout the years. Weaver et al.'s 2002 study reported that 17 percent said they expected to leave within the next five years—the same percentage as Johnstone et al., reported in 1971.

Today's Satisfaction

Determining satisfaction in the workplace is an elusive proposition. Satisfaction is an internal, individual emotional response to environmental factors. For instance, tight deadlines might fuel one journalist's perception of satisfaction while equally lowering the satisfaction of another journalist. As an emotional response, satisfaction can frequently oscillate depending on internal and external variables that assume different values. Pay, for example, had not been a constant determinant of news workers' long-term job satisfaction. However, if asked about pay, the general response was, "Sure, I wish I made more money." Previous studies have shown that salary is only a temporary solution to raising the level of satisfaction (Herzberg, 1968). Instead, for journalists, the work itself and doing good work with purpose is much more satisfying than a pay bump.

The previous research of Weaver and Wilhoit and their colleagues measured journalists' job satisfaction by asking one question: "All things considered, how satisfied are you with your present job – would you say very satisfied, fairly satisfied, somewhat dissatisfied or very dissatisfied" (Weaver and Willnat, 2014; Weaver et al., 2007, p. 264; Weaver and Wilhoit, 1996, pg. 257; Weaver and Wilhoit, 1986, p. 175).

In seeking a more reliable measurement of journalists' job satisfaction, I implemented a tool considered "the most useful and comprehensive standardized instrument" in measuring individual performance and quality of work life issues (Harrison, 1994, p. 71). A portion of the Michigan Organizational Assessment Questionnaire (Cammann et al., 1983) includes a job satisfaction variable that was established "to provide an indication of the organization members' overall affective responses to their jobs" (p. 80). The MOAQ's job satisfaction measurement has been used in dozens of studies, including the examination of white-collar employees, including editors (Chen and Spector, 1992), state government employees (Carlson and Kacmar, 2000), state civil service employees from a university (Liu, Spector, and Jex, 2005), non-faculty university employees (Jex and Gudanowski, 1992), and traffic enforcement agents (Baruch-Feldman and Schwartz, 2002).

In my research of newsroom job satisfaction since 2007, the overall levels declined in 2009 but rebounded in 2014. Throughout the studies, copy editors and page designers consistently registered the lowest levels of job satisfaction. Meanwhile, managers and columnists recorded the highest levels. From 2009 to 2014, job satisfaction among news editors and photographers reported the most noticeable changes. News editors' job satisfaction improved during that 5-year span (up 7 percent). For photographers, job satisfaction declined (down 6 percent).

News workers mired in the desk operations bore the brunt of the transitions between 2009 and 2014. As newspapers cut staff, the copy and design desks were seen as more expendable than other areas such as news editors and reporters. Universal desks—off-site locations that handle editing and design duties for an entire newspaper group—became more common, allowing for the local paper to cut or eliminate desk staff altogether. Online editing and posting responsibilities fell to the copy and design desk, as did rewriting headlines for search-engine optimization (SEO), and updating breaking news stories. Collectively, the new duties, and higher workloads because of a reduction in staff contributed to the decline in job satisfaction among copy editors and page designers.

At 37, Kathy had been a copy editor at her mid-sized newspaper her entire professional career. She had watched the copy and design desk dwindle during several rounds of layoffs. There was even talk of moving the desk operation to a centralized location along with other newspapers in the chain.

Although Kathy continued to take pride in her work, doing well became more difficult as the copy desk was downsized. "There are times when I am willing to say, 'It's good enough.' A few years ago I may have said I want to try this page a few more times. Now I say, 'It's done and there's more pages to do.'"

Kathy said that while online initiatives had been outlined, she had not embraced the online work. In fact, after speaking with several of her colleagues it was clear Kathy was in denial about her website work obligations. While admitting to not doing as she has been directed, Kathy simply said, "I see online as a necessary evil for those in the newsroom."

Throughout my research, job satisfaction in different age groups posed an interesting evolution. In the 2009 study, the youngest group (21–30 years old) of news workers were experiencing the lowest levels of job satisfaction. Meanwhile, those 51 and older demonstrated the most satisfaction. By 2014, the numbers had shifted. The 41–50 group had the lowest level while the 21–30 group and 61 and older had the highest.

In this chapter's opening, Kelly discussed her despair for the newspaper industry and of her uncertain future. When I spoke with her in 2008 she was among the under-30 crowd with the lowest levels of job satisfaction. In fact, three years after that interview she left newspapers for good. Kelly returned to college to earn a master's degree in information science. After graduation, she accepted a position at a university's medical institute as a Web project manager.

The tone among young journalists in 2014 changed dramatically. During interviews, young journalists showed an air of optimism. Working as a copy editor at a mid-sized daily, 26-year-old Connor had seen some attrition during his three years at the paper. He said the newspaper was well-respected and valued in the community, and the newsroom was making a successful transformation to producing more digital content. "(Online work is) probably night and day since I started here but that doesn't necessarily mean we're at where we should be," Connor said. "We're really trying to do more stuff on the Web. There's just so many possibilities. It doesn't feel overwhelming, but there's this huge thing to contribute to it. I think we're doing pretty well."

Amid staff cuts, increased workloads, and additional online and social media requirements, newspaper journalists have maintained high degrees of job satisfaction. When the Cammann et al's. (1983) MOAQ measurement was realigned to include a "very dissatisfied" to "very satisfied" scale, 43 percent of more than 4,600 respondents would be categorized as "very satisfied" between 2007 and 2014. Those in the "very satisfied" group dipped from 48 percent in 2007 to 42 percent in 2009, but remained relatively constant in 2014 (41 percent). The results are more akin to the 1971 Johnstone et al., study (49 percent answered "very satisfied") than the Weaver and Wilhoit studies that never exceeded 33 percent in the "very satisfied" group" (see Table 1).

Table 1 Journalists Very Satisfied With Their Jobs

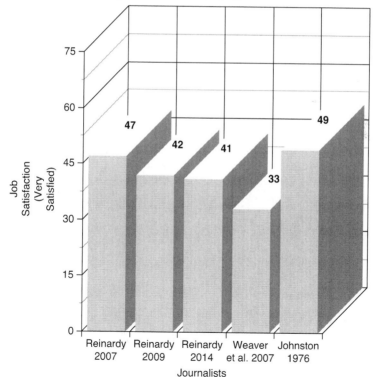

Not surprising, those experiencing burnout in my three studies (30 percent of sample) and heavier workloads (55 percent of sample) reported much lower levels of job satisfaction than the overall sample (very satisfied = 12 percent among those burned out and 35 percent for those with high rates of work overload). Also, of those intending to leave journalism (answered "yes" when asked "Do you have any intention of leaving newspaper journalism within in the next 5 years?"), only 16 percent were "very satisfied" in their work, remaining relatively consistent between 2009 (13 percent) and 2014 (15 percent).

Nonetheless, those intending to leave newspaper journalism was higher than the Weaver et al. (2007) and Johnstone et al. (1976) studies. In my 2007 study, 26 percent responded "yes" and 36 percent responded "don't know." By 2009, the number of "yes" responses dropped to 23 percent and the "no" responses rose to 44 percent. In 2014, 21 percent answered "yes" and 42 percent said "no." The "yes" answers in the previous studies of Johnston et al., (1976) and Weaver et al., (2007) did not exceed 17 percent.

Conclusions

At 46, Suzanne had worked for a mid-sized newspaper for more than half her life. As a long-time, reliable reporter she was respected in the newsroom and community. Suzanne had survived multiple rounds of staff cuts, a newspaper sale and the additional workload created by new technologies. When she started, the newsroom employed nearly 150. By 2014, the news staff had been cut to 52. Still, the standard that had been established long ago remained intact.

> I don't think that the bar has actually lowered and that, to me, is most frustrating. I don't know if anyone wants to lower it. There's this constant, "We know what we need to do but it becomes more frustrating to do it with the resources we have."

Job satisfaction for Suzanne and other journalists is determined by internal factors that remain difficult to measure. Under the traditional guise of meaningful journalism, a job well done supersedes external rewards such as monetary gain or job conditions. Even those burned out and overworked find some semblance of job satisfaction. Autonomy in work selection, appreciation by management or the public, an opportunity to make a difference in a community, and the newspaper's mission all play a role in fulfilling a newspaper worker's idea of job satisfaction (Johnstone et al., 1976; Weaver and Wilhoit, 1986; Weaver and Wilhoit, 1996; Weaver et al., 2007; Weaver and Willnat, 2014).

During my 2009 study when young journalists demonstrated the least amount of satisfaction, uncertainty of the industry and the disruption in the professional culture was troubling. But as the newsroom culture was redefined, and online and social media initiatives became normalized, by 2014 the 30 and younger journalists became the most satisfied of the groups. In fact, by 2014, holistically, job satisfaction had improved throughout the newsroom. Some of the results could be the fact that the disgruntled had left, or were asked to leave, the newspaper.

What we really learn is that even though newspapers have undergone tremendous changes—many of which were detrimental to the news worker—journalists continued to find enjoyment in what they did (see Table 2). As Suzanne said:

> I never had a desire to do something different because I still love being a reporter and still love writing stories and I still love getting the scoop. It's almost like they gotcha. It's like they know what you love to do and they take advantage of that.

Table 2 Mean Score of Journalists' Job Satisfaction in Reinardy Studies

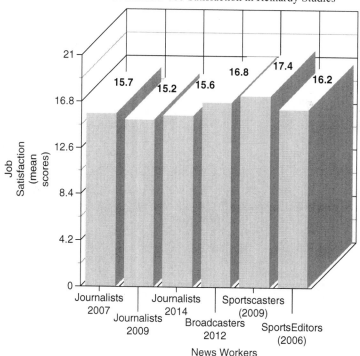

Reinardy research: Satisfaction = 3–9 low; 10–15 moderate; 16–21 high

References

Andrews, R. (1990). The concise Columbia dictionary of quotations. NY: Columbia University Press, p. 63.

Apple Employee Handbook (1993). Individual performance. Apple values. www .seanet.com/~jonpugh/applevalues.html

Baruch-Feldman, C. and Schwartz, J. (2002). Sources of social support and burnout, job satisfaction, and productivity. *Journal of Occupational Health Psychology*, 7(1): 84–93.

Cammann, C., Fichman M.G., Jenkins, Jr., D. and Klesh, J.R. (1983). Assessing the attitudes and perceptions of organizational members. In Seashore, S.E., Lawler III, E.E., Mirvis, P.H., and Cammann, C. (Eds.) *Assessing organizational change: A guide to methods, measures, practices*. NY: John Wiley.

Carlson, D.S. and Kacmar, K.M. (2000). Work-family conflict in the organization: Do life role values make a difference? *Journal of Management*, 26(5): 1031–54.

Chen, P.Y. and Spector, P.E. (1992). Relationships of work stressors with aggression, withdrawal, theft, and substance use: An exploratory study. *Journal of Occupational and Organizational Psychology*, 65(3): 177–84.

Clark, K. (1993). GM-Toyota assembly plant in California sets a standard for auto management Japanese style helps revive a failed factory. *Baltimore Sun*, September 5. http://articles.baltimoresun.com/1993-09-05/business/1993248189_ 1_nummi-assembly-plant-fremont-plant

Harrison, M.I. (1994). *Diagnosing organizations: Methods, models, and processes*. Thousand Oaks, CA: Sage Publications.

Herzberg, F. (1968). One more time: How do you motivate employees? *Harvard Business Review*, 46(1): 53–62.

Jex, S.M. and Gudanowski, D.M. (1992). Efficacy beliefs and work stress: An exploratory study. *Journal of Organizational Behavior*, 13: 509–17.

Johnstone, J.W.C., Slawski, E.J., and Bowman, W.W. (1976). *The news people: A sociological portrait of American journalists and their work*. Chicago: University of Illinois Press.

Langfitt, F. (2010). The end of the line for GM-Toyota joint venture. All Things Considered. National Public Radio. March 26. www.npr.org/templates/transcript/ transcript.php?storyId=125229157

Lee, A. M. (1937). *The daily newspaper in America: The evolution of a social instrument*. NY: The MacMillan Company.

Liu, C., Spector, P.E., and Jex, S.M. (2005). The relationship of job control with job strains: A comparison of multiple data sources. *Journal of Occupational and Organizational Psychology*, 78(3): 325–36.

Locke, E.A. (1976). The nature and causes of job satisfaction. In M.D. Dunnette (Ed.), *Handbook of industrial and organizational psychology* (pp.1297–1349). Chicago: Rand McNally.

Pfeffer, J. (1998). *The human equation: Building profits by putting people first*. Boston, Mass.: Harvard Business School Press.

Samuelson, M. (1962). A standardized test to measure job satisfaction in the news-room. *Journalism Quarterly*, 39(3), 285–91.

Schore, L. (1984). The Fremont experience: A counseling program for dislocated workers. *International Journal of Mental Health*, 13(1–2): 154–68.

Schwartz, B. (2015). *Why we work*. New York, NY: Simon & Schuster.

Weaver, D.H. and Wilhoit, G.C. (1986). *The American journalist: A portrait of U.S. news people and their work*. Bloomington, IN: Indiana University Press.

Weaver, D.H. and Wilhoit, G.C. (1996). *The American journalist in the 1990s: U.S. news people at the end of an era*. Mahwah, NJ: Lawrence Erlbaum Associates, Inc.

Weaver, D., Beam, R., Brownless, B., Voakes, P., and Wilhoit, G.C. (2007). *The American journalists in the 21st century: U.S. news people at the dawn of a new millennium*. Knight Foundation. Mahwah, NJ: Lawrence Erlbaum Associates, Inc.

Weaver, D. and Willnat, L. (2014). *The American journalists in the digital age: Key findings*. http://news.indiana.edu/releases/iu/2014/05/2013-american-journalist-key-findings.pdf.

Zimmerman, M. and Dolan, M. (2009). The end of the line for California automaking. *Los Angeles Times*, August 28. http://articles.latimes.com/2009/aug/28/business/fi-toyota-plant28

5   The New Women's Movement

Jill Abramson's firing as the *New York Times* executive editor in May 2014 re-ignited a long-standing discussion about the role of women in journalism. Media pounced on the opportunity to spotlight the conversation. "Journalism's gender problem just got worse with Jill Abramson's firing," the *New Republic* wrote a day after the dismissal (Covert, 2014). At the *Washington Post*, one headline read: "It's not just Jill Abramson: Women everywhere are getting pushed out of journalism" (Usher, 2014). The Pew Research Center posted, "As Jill Abramson exits the *NY Times*, a look at how women are faring in newsrooms" (Anderson, 2014).

Some media outlets were more direct. For instance, CNN posted, "Was Jill Abramson fired because she is a woman?" (Ghitis, 2014). And an *International Business Times* story flatly stated: "Jill Abramson's firing felt deeply among women journalists: 'We're back to square one,'" (Mintz, 2014).

Gender job inequity is not restricted to the newspaper industry. In its 2015 annual review, the U.S. Department of Labor reported that women earn on average 83 percent of what men earn (Bureau of Labor Statistics, 2015a), and only 5 percent of Fortune 500 CEOs were women (Swanson, 2015). Also, the number of women in the workforce was at its lowest level in nearly 30 years (Soergel, 2015; Bureau of Labor Statistics, 2015b).

Newspaper journalism has traditionally been a world dominated by men. In his 1898 book, *Journalism for Women: A Practical Guide*, E.A. (Arnold) Bennett wrote:

> ... there are, not two sexes, but two species – journalists and women-journalists – and that the one is about as far removed organically from the other as a dog from a cat. And we treat these two species differently. They are not expected to suffer the same discipline, nor are they judged by the same standards (p. 16).

While the number of female newsroom journalists has increased substantially since Bennett's observations (1901 census reported 9 percent of journalists were women), equality of work and pay has changed little in more than a century. In her 2013 book, *Women and Journalism*, Suzanne Franks writes: "There are still enduring stereotypes; women predominant on the lifestyle pages, but do not feature much in crime or sport. They are also far less likely to be seen on the front page ..." (p. viii).

Although women comprise 64 percent of students graduating from schools and departments of journalism and mass communications (Becker, Vlad, and Simpson, 2014) only 37 percent work in newspaper newsrooms (Jurkowitz, 2014). The 2015 American Society of News Editors' annual census reported that although 63 percent of newspapers employed at least one woman in their top three editing positions in 2014 (ASNE, 2015), over-all women in newsrooms earned about $5,000 less than men (Willnat and Weaver, 2014).

At 54 with nearly three decades of newspaper work, Sheryl was keenly aware of the gender differences in the newsroom. As a copy editor at a large newspaper (more than 100,001 circulation), job cuts and more work demands became increasingly more difficult for a woman to balance work life and home life. "The middle-age men have wives who are taking care of their lives," she said. "The women are either single or divorced, or, like me, their kids are grown."

Sheryl's assertions are supported by data I collected from newsrooms between 2007 and 2014. In 2007, 67 percent of women in the study were married. By 2014, married women in newspaper newsrooms had dropped to 52 percent. Similar declines were seen with women working in newsrooms who said they had children living at home. In 2007, 60 percent were caring for children at home but by 2014 the number had dropped to 53 percent. "It's difficult to make a living," said 49-year-old Rhiannon, a reporter who was not married and did not have children. "I think for women, if they're going to also have children and the juggling with all the extra responsibility, I don't even see how it's possible."

Gender Roles

Men and women are different, and because they are different they are indoctrinated into society under different expectations. Early sociologists operated under the premise that women were social subordinates, "unequal in their intellectual, emotional, and moral capacities" (Chafetz, 2006, p. 4). German sociologist Georg Simmel was noted for his unpopular insights into the social position of women. Simmel wrote about women's rights in the 1890s until his death in 1918 (Kandal, 1988). In his 1977 essay, "Georg Simmel's Neglected Contributions to the Sociology of Women," Lewis Coser wrote:

> (Simmel) describes the cultural and social condition that makes it extremely difficult for women to contribute to a culture that operates, by and large, according to male standards and criteria, and he shows the obstacles women face when they attempt to gain a sense of autonomous female identity in male-dominated culture (Coser, 1977, p. 871).

Eight years after his death, Karen Horney's "The Flight from Womanhood: The Masculinity-Complex in Women, as Viewed by Men and by Women" (1926) examined Simmel's "masculine civilization." Horney writes: "How far has the evolution of women, as depicted to us to-day by analysis, been measured by masculine standards and how far therefore does this picture not fail to present quite accurately the real nature of women?" (Horney, 1926, p. 100).

Gender socialization begins at birth with sex labeling and differentiation instilled by parents and caretakers, which includes specific sex language used for boys and girls, nursery décor, toys and clothing (Chafetz, 2006). Eventually, toddlers form a stable self-identity as male or female based upon these labels and actions, and then seek societal confirmation of that identity (Lewis and Weinraub, 1979; Cahill, 1983). The gender-specific identities are associated with skills traditional to females (domestic roles as caretakers, interpersonal relationships) and males (employment roles, emotional awkwardness) (Sattel, 1976).

Gender identity spills into the workplace, forcing women to resolve conflicts between home life and work life. Coser and Rokoff (1982) contend that men avoid role conflicts because of the standard expectation that prioritizes employment over family obligations. Men are traditionally breadwinners, working to support the family. For women, the obligations are flipped and women are expected to prioritize family over work. Chafetz (2006) writes: "Because of this, employers often restrict women's opportunities, women tend to have low career aspirations and they readily relinquish careers" (p. 15).

According to the U.S. Bureau of Labor Statistics, in 1970 about 38 percent of women comprised the overall labor force compared with 62 percent of men. By 2000, the number had increased to 47 percent for women, but had remained stagnate through 2014 (U.S. Department of Labor, 2015).

Women accounted for 37.2 percent of newspaper newsroom staffs in 2013, but that number fluctuated little during the previous 15 years (between 36.3 percent and 37.7 percent) (Jurkowitz, 2014). Also, the medium income for female newspaper journalists in 2012 was 83 percent of what men earned ($44,342 vs. $53,600). The wage difference held relatively steady for nearly 25 years (1991: women = 81 percent) (Willnat and Weaver, 2014).

Traditionally, men dominate the workplace. Consequently, a male-dominated hierarchy is established, which defines the norms and structure of an organization. Those norms generally re-enforce male privilege and female disadvantage (Acker, 1990; Williams, 1995; Martin, 2003; Syad and Murray, 2008). At work, women are not afforded the same advantages as men, and remain relatively disempowered (Syad and Murray, 2008). Because organizations reward a worker's physical presence demonstrated by face-time, unquestionable dedication, and those who prioritize work over other obligations such as family (Kirby et al., 2003), women do not rise to managerial positions at the same rate as men. Ackers said underlying assumptions establish gender-based work hierarchies. She wrote: "Those who are committed to paid employment are 'naturally' more suited to responsibility and authority; those who must divide their time commitments are in the lower ranks" (Acker, 1990, pp. 149–50).

For working women, there are a perceived series of obstacles that create distractions that consume their time (Acker, 1990). In a male-dominated hierarchy, those "distractions" do not mesh with the ideal norms of the work environment. Acker (1990) wrote: "Women's bodies—female sexuality, their ability to procreate and their pregnancy, breast-feeding, and child care, menstruation, and mythic 'emotionality'—are suspect, stigmatized, and used as grounds for control and exclusion" (p. 152).

The workplace for women has evolved since Acker's observations, but advancement for women has been measured, particularly in the newspaper industry. By 2013, about 35 percent of newspaper women were in supervisory roles, but that number has remained stagnant for 15 years (Jurkowitz, 2014). Not surprisingly, women make up more entry-level employees and mid-level managers than men (Chamber, Steiner, and Fleming, 2004), and generally work in areas that do not cultivate advancement (Arnold Hemlinger and Linton, 2002). And for women who left the profession, male hegemony, sex discrimination, and limited advancement opportunities were the cause (Elmore, 2007; Everbach and Flournoy, 2007; Weaver et al., 2007; Walsh-Chiders, Chance, and Herzog, 1996).

As men dominate the newsroom, particularly in managerial roles, male-centric issues shape news coverage. Female journalists embrace different ethical values than men (van Zoonen, 1998), and represent a dichotomy different than men (Fridkin, Kahn, and Goldenberg, 1991; Page, 2003;

Ross, 2002; Tuchman, 1978). While women operate in a "domestic" framework such as care and compassion, men operate in a "public sphere" such as politics and economics. When men occupy most or all of the supervisory newsroom roles, acculturation can occur throughout the newsroom, leading to unequal coverage of underrepresented groups (Shor et al., 2015). Women are expected to adopt a male news perspective. In discussing the dominance of men in newsroom roles, and the coverage produced, Shor et al. (2015) called it a "paper ceiling." In mirroring a "glass ceiling," one that limits a woman's professional advancement, a paper ceiling minimizes diversity in coverage. Shor et al. (2015) wrote:

> As long as these individuals remain overwhelmingly male, journalists' ability to make a substantial change and report equally on women and men remain limited. Put differently, as long as the real-world glass ceiling remains resistant to change, the paper ceiling of newspaper coverage is likely to remain in place (p. 977–78).

Women in Today's Newsrooms

Walking across the graduation stage to collect her journalism degree in spring 2004, Colleen realized her newspaper future was filled with possibilities. Despite professors and instructors repeatedly telling her that she'd have to start at a small newspaper and earn her way to advancement, she was offered a copy editing position at a large, reputable newspaper. "I got the job the week I graduated," Colleen said in 2016. "Actually at the time, I struck gold. 'Holy cow, I'm starting at this really big newspaper and it's amazing.' And it really was for a long time."

For most of her 11 years at the paper Colleen enjoyed entering the newsroom and doing what she loved. She survived the buyouts and layoffs, departures that had reduced the newsroom from more than 200 journalists in 2004 to about 110 by 2016. During her newspaper career, Colleen married and had two children. Eventually, she accepted a daytime position to accommodate childcare and her husband's night-time work schedule. He, too, worked at the newspaper.

Oftentimes when Colleen and her husband reached a life milestone, an unpredictable work disruption coincided. Hiring freezes and buyouts occurred about the same time they were married. In 2009, the day they closed on their first house, newspaper management announced that a quarter of the staff would be cut. Fortunately for them, Colleen and her husband kept their jobs. So, it wasn't totally unexpected that when Colleen submitted her resignation in fall 2015, the next day the newspaper announced more staff cuts. New ownership was universalizing the copy and design desks to an off-sight location. All designers were laid off, and 10 of the 20 copy editor positions were slashed.

By this time, Colleen was done with newspapers. "I was getting sick. I had headaches all the time. I was a textbook case of burnout. I was taking ibuprofen most days of the week. It was just too much." Management indicated to Colleen she would keep her job during the most recent cuts, but she might have to return to night work. She and her husband were not in a financial position to pay for childcare. Raises at the paper had been sparse and minimal. Besides, they didn't want to pay a stranger to put their children to bed at night.

There were additional concerns as well. Although she had been a loyal worker for more than a decade, and received high praise for her work, Colleen realized her home demands might not be suitable to meet the expectations of newspaper management. "They might have decided that I couldn't do the schedule that they wanted me to do and lay me off versus someone else who could work nights with no problem."

So, after 11 years, at 34, Colleen left the career she loved. She accepted a communications position with a school district. Her headaches and illness caused by stress immediately vanished. Colleen welcomed the regular hours and greater job stability, knowing she was on a structured pay system that included annual raises. Meanwhile, her husband remained at the newspaper. "We really believed in what we did but it became very apparent, as time went on, ... the right decision was to get one of our paychecks out of the newspaper world," she said. "I felt at the end I was pigeonholed. I was only doing certain things. There was so little actual editing and headline writing anymore. The creative aspects I loved about my job weren't there anymore."

Colleen identified herself as a classic burnout case, but she is not alone. As discussed in Chapter 2, newspaper women are burning out at a faster rate than men. Between 2007 and 2014, as the rate of burnout among women continued to climb, burnout among men slightly declined. Overall men and women remained in the average range for emotional exhaustion but cynicism was high, according to the Maslach Burnout Inventory-General Survey. By 2014, my studies showed that 37 percent of women were classic burnout cases (high exhaustion and cynicism) compared to 30 percent of men. However, the rate of classic burnout cases among men rose exponentially (30 percent) between 2009 and 2014 compared with women (9 percent). A possible explanation was that women who were burned out in 2009 – such as Colleen – left the newspaper industry. Meanwhile, fulfilling the role as primary breadwinner, men who were burned out remained in the newsroom. Colleen said:

> I think people are being worked to the bone and I think that there's a lot of anxiety and stress. I told (my husband) that the stress that I felt in the

spring and summer before I left, that burnout feeling, I'm beginning to see it in him too. And I think that's a common thing in most of the people at the paper.

Changing work demands and diminishing support from the organization tarnished what Colleen believed to be her dream job. Organizational support determines the level of commitment an employee has to his or her job. It measures the viability of a co-mutual relationship between the worker and his or her employer. If a worker feels he or she is treated well, the worker will be more inclined to support the organization, particularly during difficult economic or transitional times. The opposite can occur if the worker feels he or she is mistreated by an organization.

In my 2014 research, the perception of workload and organizational support for men and women had reversed. Women experienced significantly higher levels of workload than men, and lower levels of support from the organization. The role reversal can be found in the open-ended comments to the question, "If you do work differently, how so?" Job demands for women rose 9 percent between 2009 and 2014. For men, job demands remained constant during that time period. It would appear that as staff continued to shrink and job responsibilities were redistributed, the demands took a heavier toll on women than men.

Annie, a 53-year-old staff writer at a mid-sized daily, said her job changed substantially during the past few years. And as work demands increased, for her, the support system diminished.

> We are fulfilling so many jobs that other people have had in the past. That eats up a lot of time. I think we're more independent and on our own from in the past when would talk stories through and get ideas from each other. Now, I have that feeling of being isolated just because of the time demands.

Teressa, a 45-year-old graphics and photo assistant, was also experiencing the confluence of increased work demands and reduced support. She longed for the days when she started at the mid-sized newspaper, saying, "I'd just like to snap my fingers, have everything go back the way it was 20 years ago." Accepting the reality, Teressa shifted her attention to finding other employment. She said long term, she could not continue at the newspaper.

> I don't just want to work for just another company. I want to work for a place where I feel valued and I'm a part of something and it makes me

happy. I don't have the feeling of value. I feel I contribute here, but I feel I get lost a lot. A lot is expected of me but I don't feel I'm appreciated.

Sadly, Teressa was not an anomaly. When asked about intentions to leave newspapers, the percentage of women answering "yes" or "don't know" from 2007 to 2014 increased by 10 percent. In 2014, 66 percent of women were either intending to leave newspapers or were unsure (see Table 1 and Table 2).

For women under 30, the numbers were even more discouraging as 74 percent answered "yes" or "don't know" to the leaving question (35 percent = yes; 39 percent = don't know). Job demands that included more work, working faster, and Web and social media obligations accounted for 58 percent of the responses for women under 30 who were asked about working differently since starting their jobs.

The 2007 study examined the correlation between work-family conflict and the other variables. Not surprisingly, burnout and workload were contributors to conflicts between work and family expectations, but statistically in this study work-family issues did not affect women more than men.

Table 1 Percentage of Women Intending to Leave Journalism in Reinardy Studies

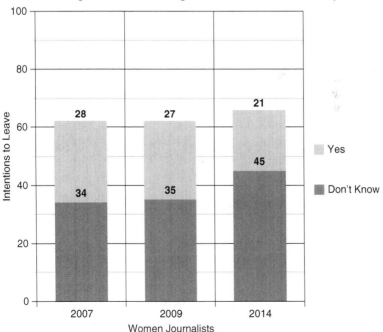

Table 2 Percentage of Men Intending to Leave Journalism in Reinardy Studies

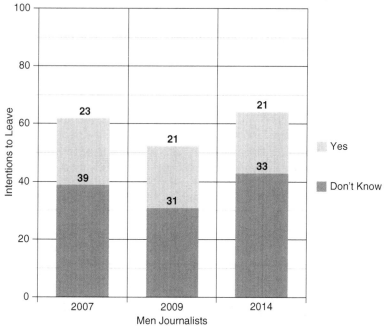

Men Journalists

Colleen said while she was at the paper, managers were accommodating to women but as work responsibilities increased following staff cuts, the juggling act became more difficult.

> There are so many demands placed on you now to work beyond your hours, to work unusual hours, to work 12-hour days. You don't feel like you can have it all as a newspaper woman. I couldn't keep doing my job and be the mom I want to be, which to me is the most important job in my life.

With so many women considering an exodus, in 2014 respondents were asked, "If you were to lose your job at the newspaper, what would you do for work?" For women 40 and younger, staying in a related field other than newspapers – magazines, online media, or freelance, was the top answer at 38 percent (compared with 31 percent of men with a similar response). The second most popular answer among women was public relations, communications, or marketing (29 percent) (25 percent for men). Pursuing educational opportunities, either returning to school or teaching, was third at 19 percent for women

(13 percent for men). Eighteen percent of women under 40 said they'd return to newspapers compared with 16 percent for men.

Interestingly, there was a clear division even among women 40 and younger. Women 27 and younger accounted for 75 percent of the "return to newspaper" responses. Public relations, communications, and marketing was the primary answer for those 28 to 40. Representing many, a 23-year-old reporter with one year of experience at a small newspaper who works 50 hours a week said, "As someone who has been laid off from newspapers before, I would do my level best to get another job at another newspaper." Several other 20-somethings said, "Find another newspaper job."

One of the most noticeable differences between men and women and their possible post-newspaper lives was found among the undecided. While 20 percent of men said they did not know what they would do if they lost their newspaper jobs, only 14 percent of women were unsure. Overall, 64 percent of men and women between 33 and 40 years old were undecided about their post-newspaper careers.

The 2014 survey also included a question about career regret. When asked, "If you could go back and choose a different career, would you?" Among women, 31 percent answered "yes" compared to 34 percent men. Thirty-one percent of women 40 and younger replied "yes" compared to 29 percent men 40 and younger. Clearly journalists working at daily newspapers continue to be a dedicated group who still find value in their work and career choice.

Conclusions

In 2012, Linda Williams Favero and Renee Guarriello Heath set out to research the generational work perspective of four generations of women who were intersecting in the current workforce. The four generations of workers included Traditionalists (born before 1945), Baby Boomers (born between 1946 and 1964), Generation X (born between 1965 and 1977), and Generation Y (born between 1978–1990). One primary finding was that the younger generations were less accepting of the traditional, male-dominated workplace. Favero and Heath (2012) wrote: "Younger generations of women in our (study) also reacted to the gendered workplace by challenging the hegemony of the discourses of paying your dues and face-time and by rejecting entitlement as an interpretive frame" (p. 350).

At 26, Kelsey was the youngest reporter at her mid-sized daily. After a couple years at another daily, she was hoping to advance her career by jumping to a larger paper. She had been in her new newsroom for two years when we spoke. "It's pointed out to me on multiple occasions I'm the token millennial," she said. "I was the first person hired after all the layoffs a few years ago. I was told I was the canary in the coal mine, which was really great to be told that after you are hired. Well, crap, that's comforting."

Kelsey's frustration with the slow transition to online and social media was palpable. "We say we're digital first," she laughed. "It's a nice catch-phrase, isn't it? I think there are some people on the online desk stuck in 1997. They're all about online but in terms of what was online 15 years ago." She said there were no staff requirements to incorporate social media into their coverage, particularly for the veteran staffers. Kelsey also said while her previous newspaper had a sense of urgency in utilizing online and social media, that wasn't the case in what was expected to be a bigger, better, and more prominent news organization. After two years, Kelsey was convinced that the current staff was unwilling or simply unable to make the transformation. She said she is left to carry the burden of online and social media initiatives without being provided the support. "Our staff is tired, no sense of urgency, coasting to retirement. I think we need some new blood or something."

Kelsey's frustration is not an aberration among young newspaper women. Research here shows that women receive less support from the organization while workload and burnout continue to increase. In addition, limited career advancement and family aspirations beyond work present a formula where women will continue to vacate newsrooms. As women depart, and a more prominent male-hegemonic culture takes root, news coverage of social and domestics issues will be affected.

Gender and role socialization begin at birth and resonate into work life. Theoretically, women assume a more caring role, prioritizing family and home obligations over work obligations. For men, the opposite is true as they are expected to be the "bread winners" and place work obligations ahead of family (Sattel, 1976; Coser and Rokoff, 1982; Chafetz, 2006).

Generally speaking, in 2014 women working in newsrooms were experiencing burnout, and two-thirds demonstrated some inclination to leave the industry. This does not bode well for an industry already depleted of women – only 37 percent – (Jurkowitz, 2014). Diversity among newsroom staffs is vital to producing news for diverse audiences (Downie and Kaiser, 2002), particularly when cultural socialization is a driving force for news. In a Nieman Report titled "Where Are the Women?" (Griffin, 2014), former *Des Moines Register* editor and former director of the USC Annenberg School of Journalism Geneva Overholser wrote: "To date, we've dutifully sought to hire 'different' folks but then forced them to conform to the reigning ethos … Folks have to quit thinking of diversity as a wearisome duty and start understanding it as a key to success …" (Overholser, 2014, p. 31).

Changing the culture, in part, resonates from leadership. However, only 35 percent of women assume supervisor roles at newspapers. Meanwhile, women opt out of the career at a higher rate than men (Jurkowitz, 2014). This study indicates that the trend will continue as women either leave the profession or work as overloaded, burned-out individuals.

In her 2013 book, *Women and Journalism*, Suzanne Franks wrote: "... women still continue to shoulder a disproportionate burden in the home (either because society expects it or they want to) which makes things harder to manage if the workplace becomes more demanding" (p. vii).

In his 1873 book, *Journalism in the United States from 1690 to 1872*, author Frederic Hudson dedicated an entire chapter to newswomen, touting their presence as editors and publishers throughout the country. Hudson was an advocate for women in the press during a time when it was still considered scandalous for a lady to work in such a tawdry business. However, Hudson wrote:

(Women) can frequently do what men can not accomplish. These female journalists, pure and bright, are the growth of the last fifteen years in America. They are now to be seen every where – in every large city where influential papers are printed (p. 504).

Under the present conditions, Hudson's 1873 vision seems less possible. Compiled with the other research and anecdotal evidence, the plight of women in newsrooms looks dire. If the current trend continues, the answer to the Nieman Report's "Where Are the Women?" seems apparent: They are not in newsrooms, and in the future they might become more difficult to find.

References

Acker, J. (1990). Hierarchies, jobs, bodies: A theory of gendered organizations. *Gender & Society*, 4(2): 139–58.

Anderson, M. (2014). As Jill Abramson exits the *NY Times*, a look at how women are faring in newsrooms. Pew Research Center, May 16. www.pewresearch.org/fact-tank/2014/05/16/as-jill-abramson-exits-the-ny-times-a-look-at-how-women-are-faring-in-newsrooms/

Arnold Hemlinger, M. and Linton, C.C. (2002). *Women in newspapers 2002: Still fighting an uphill battle*. Evanston, IL: Media Management Center, Northwestern University in partnership with the Robert R. McCormick Tribune Foundation.

ASNE (2015). 2015 Census. Percentage of minorities in newsrooms remains relatively steady; 63 percent of newspapers have at least one woman among top-three editors. July 28. http://asne.org/content.asp?pl=121&sl=415&contentid=415

Becker, L., Vlad, T., and Simpson, H.A. (2014). *2013 Annual survey of journalism & mass communication enrollment*. Aug. 6. Retrieved Oct. 20, 2014, from: www.grady.uga.edu/annualsurveys/Enrollment_Survey/Enrollment_2013/2013Enroll Combined.pdf

Bennett, E.A. (1898). *Journalism for women: A practical guide*. London: J. Lane.

Bureau of Labor Statistics (2015a). Women's earnings compared to men's earnings in 2014. U.S. Department of Labor. November 30. www.bls.gov/opub/ted/2015/womens-earnings-compared-to-mens-earnings-in-2014.htm

Bureau of Labor Statistics (2015b). Labor force statistics from the current population survey. U.S. Department of Labor. February 12. www.bls.gov/cps/lfcharacteristics.htm#laborforce

Cahill, S. (1983). Re-examining the acquisition of sex roles: A symbolic interactionist approach. *Sex Roles*, 9: 1–15.

Chafetz, J.S. (2006). *Handbook of the sociology of gender*. New York: Springer-Science+Business Media.

Chambers, D., Steiner, L., and Fleming, C. (2004). *Women and journalism*. New York: Routledge.

Coser, L.A. (1977). Georg Simmel's neglected contributions to the sociology of women. *Signs*, 2(4): 869–76.

Coser, R.L., and Rokoff, G. (1982). Women in the occupational world: Social disruption and conflict. *Social Problems*, 18: 535–54.

Covert, B. (2014). Journalism's gender problem just got worse with Jill Abramson's firing. *New Republic*, May 15. www.newrepublic.com/article/117769/jill-abramsons-firing-and-gender-pay-gap-american-journalism

Downie, L., and Kaiser, R.G. (2002). *The news about the news: American journalism in peril*. New York: Alfred A. Knopf.

Elmore, C. (2007). Recollections in hindsight from women who left: The gendered newsroom culture. Women and Language, 30(2): 18–27.

Everbach, T. and Flournoy, C. (2007). Women leave journalism for better pay, work conditions. *Newspaper Research Journal*, 28(3): 52–64.

Favero, L.W. and Heath, R.G. (2012). Generational perspectives in the workplace: Interpreting the discourses that constitute women's struggle to balance work and life. *Journal of Business Communication*, 49(4): 332–56.

Franks, S. (2013). *Women and journalism*. New York: I.B. Tauris & Co.

Fridkin Kahn, K. and Goldenberg, E.N. (1991). Women candidates in the news: An examination of gender differences in U.S. Senate campaign coverage. *Public Opinion Quarterly*, 55(2): 180–99.

Ghitis, F. (2014). Was Jill Abramson fired because she is a woman? CNN.com, May 16. http://www.cnn.com/2014/05/15/opinion/ghitis-jill-abramson-firing/

Griffin, A. (2014). Where are all the women? *Nieman Reports*, 68(3): 28–43.

Horney, K. (1926). The flight from womanhood: The masculinity-complex in women, as viewed by men and by women. *International Journal of Psychoanalysis*, 7: 324–329. Found in *Female Sexuality: Contemporary Engagements*, (1999). Donna Bassin, editor, North Bergen, N.J.: Book-mart Press.

Hudson, F. (1873). *Journalism in the United States from 1690 to 1872*. New York: Harper & Brothers, Publishers.

Jurkowitz, M. (2014). ASNE: Two-thirds of U.S. newspapers employ women in top editing jobs. Pew Research Center, July 30. http://www.pewresearch.org/fact-tank/2014/07/30/asne-two-thirds-of-u-s-newspapers-employ-women-in-top-editing-jobs/

Kandal, T.R. (1988). *The women question in classical sociological theory*. Miami: Florida International University Press.

Kirby, E.L., Golden, A.G., Medved, C.E., Jorgenson, J., and Buzzanell, P.M. (2003). An organizational communication challenge to the discourse of work and family research: From problematics to enpowerment. In P.J. Kalbfleisch (Ed.), *Communication yearbook* 27: 1–43. Thousand Oaks, CA: Sage.

Lewis, M. and Weinraub, M. (1979). Origins of early sex-role development. *Sex Roles*, 5: 135–53.

Martin, P.Y. (2003). "Said and done" versus "saying and doing": Gendering practices, practicing gender at work. *Gender & Society*, 17: 342–66.

Mintz, Z. (2014). Jill Abramson's firing felt deeply among women journalists: "We're back to square one." *International Business Times*, May 15. http://www.ibtimes .com/jill-abramsons-firing-felt-deeply-among-women-journalists-were-back-square-one-1585049

Overholser, G. (2014). Geneva Overholser: Former editor, *The Des Moines Register*. *Nieman Reports*, 68(3): 31.

Page, R.E. (2003). "Cherie: Lawyer, wife mum:" Contradictory patterns of representation in media reports of Cherie Booth/Blair. *Discourse & Society*, 14(5): 559–79.

Ross, K. (2002). *Women, politics, media: Uneasy relations in comparative perspective*. Cresskill, NJ: Hampton Press.

Sattel, J. (1976). The inexpressive male: Tragedy or sexual politics? *Social Problems*, 23–4: 469–477.

Shor, E., van de Rijt, A., Miltsov, A., Kulkarni, V., and Skiena, S. (2015). A paper ceiling: Explaining the persistent underrepresentation of women in printed news. *American Sociological Review*, 80(5): 960–84.

Soergel, A. (2015). Where are all the workers? *U.S. News & World Report*. July 16. www.usnews.com/news/the-report/articles/2015/07/16/unemployment-is-low-but-more-workers-are-leaving-the-workforce

Swanson, A. (2015). The number of Fortune 500 companies led by women is at an all-time high: 5 percent. *The Washington Post*. June 4. www.washingtonpost .com/news/wonk/wp/2015/06/04/the-number-of-fortune-500-companies-led-by-women-is-at-an-all-time-high-5-percent/

Syad, J. and Murray, P.A. (2008). A cultural feminist approach towards managing diversity in top management teams. *Equal Opportunity International*, 27(5): 413–32.

Tuchman, G. (1978). The symbolic annihilation of women in the mass media. In *Hearth and Home: Images of Women in the Mass Media*, eds. Gaye Tuchman, Arelen Kaplan Daniels, and James Benet. NY: Oxford University Press: 3–38.

U.S. Department of Labor (2015). Data & statistics: Women in the labor force. March. www.dol.gov/wb/stats/stats_data.htm.

Usher, N. (2014). It's not just Jill Abramson: Women everywhere are getting pushed out of journalism. *The Washington Post*, May 28. www.washingtonpost.com/posteverything/wp/2014/05/28/its-not-just-jill-abramson-women-everywhere-are-getting-pushed-out-of-journalism/

Van Zoonen, L. (1998). One of the girls? The changing gender of journalism. In *News, Gender, and Power*, eds. Cynthia Carter, Gill Branston, and Stuart Allan. London and New York: Routledge: 33–46.

Walsh-Childers, K., Chance, J., and Herzog, K. (1996). Women journalists report discrimination in newsrooms. *Newspaper Research Journal*, 17(3–4): 68–87.

Williams, C. (1995). *Still a man's world: Men who do "women's" work*. Berkeley, CA: University of California Press.

Weaver, D., Beam, R., Brownless, B., Voakes, P., and Wilhoit, G.C. (2007). *The American journalists in the 21st century: U.S. news people at the dawn of a new millennium*. Knight Foundation. Mahwah, NJ: Lawrence Erlbaum Associates, Inc.

Willnat, L. and Weaver, D. (2014). *The American journalist in the digital age: Key findings*. http://news.indiana.edu/releases/iu/2014/05/2013-american-journalist-key-findings.pdf

6 A New "Social Responsibility"

With freedom comes responsibility. For newspaper journalists, responsibility is founded on the bedrock of democracy, outlined in newsroom mission statements and enforced by a culture entrusted to produce truthful, comprehensive, and fair information.

Protected by the First Amendment and consecrated by the group known as the Hutchins Commission (The Commission on Freedom of the Press, 1947), a journalist's social responsibility serves the political system, enlightens the public, and safeguards individual liberties. Newspapers are commissioned with fostering "Great Communities" of civil engagement and action (Baran and Davis, 2015, p. 73). How well those "Great Communities" are served in light of early 21st century newspaper transformations remains an open question. Newspaper staffs were cut by more than 33 percent; layoff survivors are asked to do more work (social media, online, etc.) with fewer resources. The new newsroom cultivated an environment of job insecurity and fear. As a result, the fear solidifies the status quo of news production while minimizing innovation and change (Ekdale et al., 2014).

With what has transpired during the past decade, newspaper journalism no longer resembles what Hutchins or even the Founding Fathers had imagined. Technology has afforded the freedom to anyone with a computer and Internet access to act as a journalist—but not necessarily act under the guise of journalistic responsibility. And while newspaper journalists are provided more autonomy through social media to reach more and different audiences, the traditional tenets of good, responsible journalism become untethered. Oftentimes news workers are given the responsibility to tweet, blog, and post at their discretion with little to no organizational gatekeeping.

In this new age of newspaper journalism, the social responsibility component has changed dramatically. And although news workers continue to embrace the tenets of social responsibility (acting as a local source for news, informing the community, and providing a watchdog service), fulfilling the mission has become far more complex. In an era when being social is more accessible than any time in human history, being responsible becomes an unintended casualty. Too often, speed trumps editing and even fact checking.

With the Internet, communities have become more expansive, diverse, and demanding than ever before. Meanwhile, newsroom staffs are the smallest they've been in more than 35 years. In a configuration where something has to give, ultimately social responsibility might become little more than the idealistic notion of scholars and academics. Despite the commitment of news workers to inform, educate, and engage the community, social responsibility could be on the cusp of becoming another casualty of the daily demands of a 21st century newspaper.

The Fourth Estate

During an address to the British House of Commons in the late 1700s, Irish Statesman Edmund Burke gave credence to the press' role as the bedrock to a democratic system. In his 1859 book, Thomas Carlyle wrote:

> Burke said there were Three Estates in Parliament; but, the Reporters' Gallery yonder, there sat a *Fourth Estate* (Carlyle's italics) more impor-tant than they all. ... Printing which comes necessarily out of Writing, I say often, is equivalent to Democracy: invent Writing, Democracy is inevitable (p. 147).

The Internet gives the appearance that the Fourth Estate has grown exponen-tially. Worldwide transmission of electronic information seems emblematic of the marketplace of ideas; however, it does not account for the reliability, substance, or validity of that information.

American journalism has tussled with freedom and responsibility since its inception. But in 1942, magazine mogul Henry Luce (*Time, Life, Fortune, Sports Illustrated* to name a few) commissioned University of Chicago Chancellor Robert Hutchins to form a committee that would examine "the present and future prospects of the freedom of the press" (The Commission on Freedom of the Press, 1947, p. v). Five years and $215,000 later the com-mission issued its report. In the forward of *A Free and Responsible Press*, Hutchins wrote:

> This report deals with the responsibilities of the owners and managers of the press to their consciences and the common good for the formation of public opinion. It goes without saying that the responsibilities of the owners and managers of the press for American culture are as great as those outlined in this report (p. vi).

The commission outlined five requirements of the press:

- A truthful, comprehensive, and intelligent account of the day's events in a context which gives them meaning
- A forum for the exchange of comment and criticism
- A means of projecting the opinions and attitudes of groups in the society to one another
- A method of presenting and clarifying the goals and values of the society
- A way of reaching every member of the society by the currents of information, thought, and feeling which the press supplies. (The Commission on Freedom of the Press, 1947, pp. 20–21).

The report rang hollow with the popular press. In his review, Yale Law Professor Ralph Brown wrote in the *Faculty Scholarship Series* (1948): "They (the Commission) could have provoked great debate. They did not. The Luce press, naturally, gave the Report a big play. The rest of the press threw rocks at it" (p. 894).

Although the Commission's report did little to inspire the press, contrary to Brown's assertions, it did provoke debate. Nine years later, Siebert, Peterson, and Schramm (1956) adopted the principles outlined by the Hutchins Commission in their development of social responsibility theory. The Commission's five responsibilities bore out of the notion that the First Amendment is not enough to guarantee citizens an equal opportunity to say what they desire to say, particularly when press owners and managers determine which facts, which version of events, and what ideas will reach the public domain. Siebert et al. wrote:

> This uneasiness is the basis of developing Social Responsibility theory: that the power and near monopoly position of the media impose on them the obligation to be socially responsible, to see that all sides are fairly presented and that the public has enough information to decide; and that if the media do not take on themselves such responsibility it may be necessary for some other agency of the public to enforce it (p. 5).

Although the Hutchins report was the catalyst for social responsibility theory, Siebert et al. (1956) were adamant that responsible publishers, editors, and reporters had long established the essentials of the theory. The theory's major premise: media that operate under a "privileged position" in the government is mutually obligated to society in providing essential functions. Siebert et al. wrote that social responsibility theory "accepts the role of the press in servicing the political system, in enlightening the public, in safeguarding the liberties of the individual; but it represents the opinion that the press has been deficient in performing those tasks" (p. 74). While acknowledging the role as a for-profit enterprise, economics should not take precedence over informing and educating the public, serving as a watchdog of government, or providing a forum for discussion and debate (Siebert et al., 1956).

The tenets of a free and responsible media have been extensively debated. Scholars have argued that media autonomy and freedom from government are secondary to its freedom to provide a responsible service to citizens. Others contend that 70 years of social responsibility have created communitarianism—a political and social philosophy where community connection, engagement, and common good supersedes individualism and economics. Some contend that social responsibility led to community boosterism in lieu of a community watchdog.

Social responsibility was revitalized during the "civic" or "public" journalism movement of the 1990s. Civic journalism was intended to engage, inform, and encourage citizens to actively participate in their communities. A 1995 joint report by the Pew Center for Civic Journalism and the Poynter Institute for Media Studies stated, "Citizens who don't participate in the life of their community have little need for news. Civic journalism seeks to address some of this detachment and improve journalism in a way that may help stimulate civic discourse" (Civic Journalism: Six Case Studies, 1995, p. 1).

Civic journalism marked a more active role for journalistic social responsibility, holding media accountable in engaging and assisting public life (Gade, Abel, Antecol, Hsueh, Hume, Morris, Packard, Willey, Fraser, and Sanders, 1998). In their study of two mid-sized newspapers, Gade et al. (1998) concluded that civic journalism had expanded social responsibility but the journalism is not "a drastic departure from past practice." However, news workers were willing to experiment with "new ways that allow the media to respond to a changing society" (p. 24).

At the cusp of the great newsroom exodus beginning in 2006, public journalism began to fade but left an impression. In analyzing 15 years of research, Nip (2008) identified six major practices of public journalism, including several that mirror the Hutchins Commission report of 60 years earlier:

- Giving ordinary people a voice (Hutchins: a means of projecting the opinions and attitudes of groups in the society to one another)
- Covering stories in a way that facilitates public understanding and stimulates citizen deliberation of the problems behind the story (Hutchins: a truthful, comprehensive, and intelligent account of the day's events in a context which gives them meaning)
- Presenting news to make it more accessible and easier for people to engage in the issues (Hutchins: a method of presenting and clarifying the goals and values of the society) (Nip, 2008, p. 180).

Professional Calling

It has been said that journalism is a noble profession practiced by those of high integrity. It's a passionate calling for some, similar to the ministry or social work. Universally, accurately reporting the news, informing the public, providing balanced coverage of events, and acting as a governmental watchdog are accepted journalistic obligations. Journalists are proud of their work, find excitement in the job, and as historian, journalist, and Pulitzer Prize winner Frank Luther Mott (1962) suggested, include those of professional spirit, based upon "devotion to service … attention to the adequate preparation of its practitioners … and adherence to certain standards. In theory, the professional man places service above personal gain" (p. 863).

In light of new and different work obligations of 21st century journalism, service above personal gain is redefined. Changes in the newspaper industry forced workers to work differently, produce content on their off time (Deuze 2007; Robinson 2011), sacrifice quality for quantity (Reinardy, 2010), and lose autonomy in their work (Willnat and Weaver 2014).

However, commitment to the calling had not subsided. In three different studies I conducted between 2007 and 2014 involving nearly 4,000 newspaper journalists, the average hours worked per week exceeded the standard 40 hours in each study. In fact, journalists in the 2014 study said they worked on average 46 hours per week and 40 percent said they worked more than that. In 2009, 33 percent said they worked more than 46 hours per week. By comparison, journalists in 2014 worked longer than news workers reported in any of my previous research. The commitment to the journalistic cause appeared to remain strong, at least in terms of allocation of time effort.

The social responsibility function of the press provides a professional purpose that allows journalists to feel they contribute to the betterment of society. It allows them to function outside the economic realities of the industry. It enables them to freely report on controversial issues because it's socially responsible to do so, unencumbered by the perspective that they are beholden to influential parties. Social responsibility also shields journalists from government interference, and provides the autonomy to hold others responsible (Altschull, 1995). Altschull (1995) writes: "… there remains for the individual journalist the possibility of performing important services for the public—and, more significant, the possibility of uniting institutionally with his or her colleagues to help change the course of human history" (p. 446).

In a healthy newsroom, journalists rally around the social responsibility described in the newspaper's mission statement. Although the words formalize the newspaper's function, it's the spirit behind the words that motivate the news workers. Management relies upon newsroom social responsibility to get more from its workers, oftentimes without paying overtime. It creates an environment of commitment to a greater purpose instead of commitment to self. And, social responsibility inspires journalists to produce good work.

Although newspapers capitalize on journalistic dedication, it's a self-inflicted, long-established condition perpetuated by news workers. Saying "no" to an assignment or longer hours or more work is detrimental to career development. The societal commitment, however, runs deeper than merely professional progress. In part, university journalism education is steeped in traditional rhetoric about obligation to community, and "shedding light into dark places." The Watergate work of Woodward and Bernstein continues to be a call to action for young journalists.

Traditionally, long-standing newsroom culture and practices indoctrinate new hires into doing journalism "the right way." Through osmosis, observation, and directives, new workers learn the culture of producing journalism of and for the community in the tradition established by that particular newsroom. In light of diminished newsroom staffs, the priority of the old guard to impart the culture and expectations to the new guard has eroded. Coupled with new, more, and different work, the culture is rapidly shifting away from a traditional expectation of journalism to a modern one. Simply reporting the day's events in the morning edition is no longer acceptable. The news is immediate and constant, variables that the traditional newsroom has been slow to account for or incorporate into its culture.

The New "Social"

It's no revelation that the work of newspaper journalists has changed dramatically in recent years. The reduction in print circulation, declining advertising revenues, and the expansion of online readership has substantially altered the workload and the staff size of newspaper newsrooms. Doing more with less has become a commonality for news workers. Real-time Web traffic analysis tests the maximum limits of content production and acts as a constant reminder that the concept of deadline is fluid and not absolute.

Newsroom staffers are at the epicenter of this journalistic maelstrom. News workers are expected to carefully consider audience expectations (print, online, social media, words, visuals, interactivity), time investment vs. outcomes, and the purpose—social and economic—of the work being conducted.

Newsrooms feature large TV monitors that track Web traffic, enticing reporters and editors to watch stories spike online after being posted. Management issues hourly, daily, or weekly memos with the latest online numbers, doling out kudos to those whose have the most popular Web stories of the week. Meanwhile, reporters turn quick and quirky stories to snag online trollers, knowing they'll be rewarded—at least publicly—for their single-sourced, oddity story.

After 24 years as a reporter, Sue had also fallen victim to the Web traffic board. Although she scrolled the traffic reports each day, she grew to dislike its purpose. "It depresses me. When I look at the body of my work over a year and the top 100 most read stories during the year … I go after stories now because I think they'll be big online. Stories I might not have gone after before."

Sue told a story of an abandoned car on a major traffic way for several days that was receiving some attention on Twitter. Suddenly, she was compelled to get the story. "It was stupid and not related to anything I'd write, but I knew judging from Twitter traffic that it would be an interesting, light-hearted story online, and it was. I do those stories now without thinking."

After the story was posted, it was an online sensation for the paper. Clicks soared and Sue was applauded for her efforts. Although she resents the "low-hanging fruit" journalism, Sue saw a bright side. "It's nice to be able to count the numbers and see how many people are reading it. Before it was always a mystery."

It's not uncommon for the newsroom Web traffic board to influence the daily news decisions. Producing for social media or the online site greatly influence news production in terms of content and quality. In these studies, when journalists were asked, "Since starting in your newsroom, do you work differently?" Among nearly 3,500 respondents, 75 percent answered "yes." In 2009, 68 percent of news workers answered "yes." By 2014, that number had jumped to 83 percent.

In some cases, the Web-tracking TV monitors have great influence in news production. After spending a week in one small newspaper (less than 50,000 circulation) it was clear, in part, what was driving the news, particularly among the reporting staff that numbered about 15.

During interviews in 2014, the predominant conversation regarding the online objective focused on getting breaking news online quickly, the struggle to find balance between producing online content and newspaper content, and the daily Web traffic reports provided by management. Online analytics had generated an awareness of not only online traffic but online staff production. There was a basic understanding that the website was part and parcel of the daily news reporting, and an understanding that, for better or worse, online work carried significance and importance. That duality was summarized in one staffer's comment: "There are pressures in the news-room to produce traffic. Analytics are important and stressed at times … but I also think there's a danger in that to do things only because of the traffic." Another journalist in that newsroom said:

> I don't want to say (managers) are click driven because I think they're journalism driven, but they're very tuned in and very aware of online readership, social media and driving Web traffic. It's hard not to feel

it's important because your superiors are telling you it's critical to have online readers. If you are not getting clicks you're not doing your job.

In the newsroom, there was a clear division between the younger and more experienced staffers. Younger journalists said they sometimes "chased clicks" by writing quick, easy stories they knew would generate traffic. One said, "There are times where traffic is slow at some particular point of the day and you brainstorm something to throw up, not necessarily to get clicks or to get traffic but something that might be interesting."

Another said: "It almost becomes a game in-and-of-itself. 'OK, there's only 190 people. Let me think of a blog that might get some interest and have some fun and provide some entertainment value. I'll post it, and in an hour check to see where our traffic is. Is it at 380? Did I double it? You don't chase the clicks but you chase the adrenalin of bringing people to your site."

There were a group of reporters in this newsroom who said there was awareness and even competition to drive Web traffic, and understood that doing so clashed with the notions of producing good journalism. One said: "I'd say there's a little bit of competition because no one wants to be the least-read person here."

At that newspaper, management's daily click logs included congratulations to those generating the most traffic, regardless of work effort or quality of work. Many reporters said they didn't "clickbait"—providing a sensational headline to lure readers into a story—but realized the newsroom implications of not luring an audience. Web analytics affected pay raises, promotions, and story assignments.

One reporter with 30-plus years experience explained how he dedicated a couple days of reporting and writing an interesting human-interest story that was featured in the newspaper. He said he became frustrated because the story did not receive the attention from readers or management as expected. At about the same time he spent 20 minutes writing a quick and easy gossip blog that received tons of clicks and praise from management. "(The feature) didn't get enough clicks for what it was worth and (the blog) got way too many for what it was worth. A lot time spent for the amount of clicks; very little time for the amount of clicks. You've got to do what you've got to do." The reporter admitted that he generates "eye candy" stories to pump up his click count to satisfy management.

In subsequent organizational ethnographical studies in three additional mid-sized newsrooms (circulation 50,001–100,001), similar practices emerged but not to the same extent. Although journalists in other newsrooms did not always talk about "chasing clicks," the online and social media objectives outlined by management were clear—reach the audience in different platforms and distribute the news as quickly as possible. A primary concern in all the newsrooms involved in my research was the influence of online and social media objectives on traditional practices in producing quality, depth, and accurate journalism. Newspaper news workers were keenly aware of multiple audiences as circulation had become only one measurement of success. And while the shift to additional platforms was recognized, acknowledged, and mostly embraced by journalists, online and social media created additional challenges in the journalistic process.

Meeting the Mission

Mission statements outline a company's core goals and values. Mission statements provide a general organizational guide for employees as they conduct their daily work. But as with all guiding principles, mission statements outline an overarching tone while allowing for case-by-case consideration. For example, the American Society of News Editors mission statement reads:

> The American Society of News Editors is dedicated to the leadership of American journalism. It is committed to fostering the public discourse essential to democracy; helping editors maintain the highest standards of quality, improve their craft, and better serve their communities; and preserving and promoting core journalistic values, while embracing and exploring change. (ASNE, 1994).

Mission statements oftentimes are filled with subjective language—"highest standards of quality;" "better serve their communities;" "preserving and promoting core journalistic values." Although agreement can be found among phrase subjectivity, the goals would be malleable to specific newspapers and communities. The "highest standard of quality" might be substantially different between the *New York Times* and *The Podunk Times*.

Nearly every newspaper newsroom has a mission statement. All are stated in employee handbooks, many are posted on the newspapers' websites, and some are even etched into newsroom walls. The journalistic mission professes the responsibility set forth to those expected to fulfill it. Generally speaking, the guiding principles of newspaper mission statements include providing an account of the day's events, relaying important community stories, speaking for those who have little voice, telling people what to think about, and providing a historical account for future generations. Rarely, if ever, do newspaper mission statements mention profit margins or news investment.

In interviews with nearly 100 newspaper workers, the most common word they used to describe their newspapers' mission statement included "community"—to serve it, be a watchdog for it, tell the stories of it, and to inform it. Many described a renewed emphasis on local news coverage in recent years. A 25-year-old copy editor said:

> I think the mission should be the source for local news. When I first got here there were a lot of wire pages and the paper was a lot bigger. There was a lot of nation, state, and world stuff. We had a meeting where we're like we're going to be more local and make the paper smaller and put more local content in it.

The commitment to community service was nearly universal among journalists interviewed. One 36-year-old reporter summed it up:

> We're not only the watchdog of the community but the voice of the community. People can come to us for reliable and interesting and entertaining information from across all walks of life. Taking that responsibility seriously is the No. 1 role of any newspaper and I love that we have this little niche.

A 30-year veteran and metro editor described her newspaper's mission as a social responsibility, saying:

> I think we think our mission is to get answers, to investigate things. We feel we have a public responsibility. Often we're writing stories and looking into things that nobody would look into or get answers to. Public service, I guess.

Newspaper journalists continued to embrace the idea that they were the "go-to" source for news in the community, although admitted the audience is fractured and isn't as dedicated to the newspaper as it once had been. The sense of value and worth of the newspaper in the community had been diminished through online competition and the public perception that the newspaper wasn't what it used to be in terms of quality and quantity. News workers said while they are still committed to their newspaper's mission, online and social media efforts made achieving the mission much more difficult. In addition, self-selection of news among audience members created a love-hate relationship with online entities. Journalists loved the fact that analytics provided evidence of how attractive stories, photos, videos, and other items were to readers. They hated the fact that news self-selection created more competition, and their work might never be seen by readers.

When asked, "How well does your newspaper fulfill its mission?" among nearly 100 journalists interviewed, almost all said their newspaper was doing well in fulfilling the mission but not as well as in the past. Primarily, the reduction in resources and increase in online workload accounted for the mission going unfulfilled. Representing many journalists, a 38-year-old copy editor who had been at his newspaper for nine years, said:

> Some things have declined over the years because of the shrinkage of the newspaper and the staff. There's no way you can keep up with the level of newspaper from a few years ago with a much smaller staff and many more sections. But I think the people who are still here are dedicated to doing their job well. We do as well as we can, given those circumstances.

Many of the conversations about mission fulfillment turned to the idea of not being able to blanket cover the community as well as in the past. All the journalists interviewed were working in newsrooms that had experienced 40 to 60 percent reduction in newsroom staffs. A 41-year-old news editor with 14 years experience at his newspaper said:

> Knowing what we did before, it's hard to say we do it as well as we used to. I think we do a good job with what we have left. I think the people here are good journalists and strive hard to do the best that they can every day. That said, I don't feel we have the resources to do the best job we possibly can and to do that mission as well as we could.

For a majority of those interviewed, there remains a great pride in what they accomplished each day, but it's bittersweet. They recognized what is done today is not nearly the journalism—in depth and breadth—as it once was. Representing the sentiments of several news workers, a 45-year-old editor with 26 years at the paper said:

> Given the current economic times and the state of the industry and the limitations, I don't think we can cover the community as well as we possibly could and should. If you look at our staff it's a shell of what it once was and there's no way we can cover things the way we used to. Unfortunately, things get lost in the shuffle.

A 35-year-old reporter with 15 years experience at the paper said the paper was doing well fulfilling the mission but, "We're not as thorough, we're not as far-reaching, we are not as responsive as we used to be. I think (because) the crunch to get a lot of things done with far fewer people, we aren't physically capable of doing as much as we used to."

The major theme among newspaper workers was that they were doing the best they could with what they had. There remained a sense of purpose in providing vital news and information to the community. However, as the news workers' commitment remained constant under the circumstances, there was an understanding among them that their newspaper's relevance was moderated. Regardless of how hard or fast they worked, newspaper news workers could not reach the same standard of work as in the past.

Conclusions

The social responsibility adopted by U.S. newspapers was cultivated in the First Amendment, nurtured by passionate journalists fostering great communities, and re-enforced by movements such as those initiated by the Hutchins' Commission and civic journalism. However, in light of new technologies news is being developed in different forms (blogs, videos, social media, etc.) for a variety of platforms (computer, smartphones, etc.). "Social" has expanded the audience exponentially beyond the dead-tree readers who retrieve their version of news from the driveway or doorstep each morning.

As newspaper journalists continued to embrace the notions of social responsibility (acting as a local source for news, informing the community, and providing a watchdog service), fulfilling the mission had become far more complex. Although journalists predominantly agreed that the social responsibility mission was being met, it wasn't being met as well as in the past because of reduction in resources, and new and different work responsibilities brought on by staff cuts and digital initiatives.

News workers remained committed to the idealism of social responsibility, but reality intervenes. The sense of contributing to the greater good of the community is genuine. The means to do so is more complex. Long-standing newsroom traditions had been fractured. In the past, newsroom veterans indoctrinated new employees into the newsroom culture and traditions. A historical standard had been established and passed down to each generation. As 40 to 60 percent of staffs were cut, veterans did not have the time or inclination to instruct new workers. Besides, with online and social media demands, and the pressure of Web analytics, the newsroom traditions were in flux.

During times of change, organizations prepare for change, initiate change, and then re-establish a new culture. Some established practices survive the change and remain an intricate aspect of the new culture. Others are discarded completely, causing great consternation among those resisting the change.

As newsrooms re-establish their culture, journalists recognize that work routines and practices are drastically different. Throughout the chaos of change, certain absolutes are maintained as a framework for rebuilding. For instance, at newspapers the idea of the deadline still prevails; however, actual deadlines are completely different. Deadlines are no longer constant but fluid and continuous. Still, journalists are expected to meet deadlines, whatever they might be.

The same can be said for the newspaper's social responsibility mission. As the established mission has survived the newsroom transformation and audience expectations, fulfilling it creates far more challenges. Among the challenges, journalists are torn between a high level of production, satisfying audience wants and needs, and trying to serve their communities. While not mutually exclusive, rectifying all those challenges is complex and sometimes confusing. For some journalists, meeting the social responsibility obligations under the current demands might be improbable. Reaching the same standard of social responsibility as in the past might even be impossible.

References

Altschull, J.H. (1995). *Agents of power: The media and public policy.* White Plains, N.Y.: Longman Publishers.

ASNE, 1994. Mission statement. September. http://asne.org/content.asp?pl=24&sl= 32&contentid=32.

Baran, S.J. and Davis, D.K. (2015). *Mass communication theory: Foundations, ferment, and future,* 7th edition. Stamford, CT: Cengage Learning.

Brown, R.S. (1948). The commission of the press, A free and responsible press: A general report on mass communication, newspapers, radio, motion pictures, magazines and books. Yale Law School Faculty Scholarship Series. January 1: 892–901.

Carlyle, T. (1859). *On heroes, hero-worship, and the heroic in history.* NY: John Wiley.

Civic Journalism: Six Case Studies (1995). A joint report by the Pew Center for civic journalism and the Poynter Institute for Media Studies, July, 1.

Deuze, Mark. 2007. *Media work.* Malden, MA: Polity Press.

Ekdale, B., Tully, M., Harmsen, S., and Singer, J.B. (2014). Newswork within a culture of job insecurity: Producing news amidst organizational and industry uncertainty. *Journalism Practice,* Oct. 8. DOI: 10.1080/17512786.2014.963376.

Gade, P., Abel, S., Antecol, M., Hsueh, H-Y, Hume, J., Morris, J., Packard, A., Willey, S., Fraser, N., and Sanders, K. (1998). Journalists' attitudes toward civic journalism media roles. *Newspaper Research Journal,* 19(4): 10–26.

Mott, F.L. (1962). *American journalism: A history: 1690–1960.* NY: The McMillan Company.

Nip, J.Y.M. (2008). The last days of civic journalism: The case of the *Savannah Morning News. Journalism Practice,* 2(2): 179–96.

Reinardy, S. (2010). Downsizing effects on personnel: The case of layoff survivors in U.S. newspapers. *Journal of Media Business Studies,* 7(4): 1–19.

Robinson, S. (2011). "Journalism as process": The organizational implications of participatory online news. *Journalism & Communication Monographs* 13: 137–210.

Siebert, F.S., Peterson, T., and Schramm, W. (1956). *Four theories of the press.* Chicago, Ill: University of Illinois Press.

The Commission on Freedom of the Press (1947). *A free and responsible press.* Chicago, Ill: The University of Chicago Press.

Willnat, L., and Weaver, D. (2014). *The American journalist in the digital age: Key findings.* http://news.indiana.edu/releases/iu/2014/05/2013-american-journalist-key-findings.pdf.

7   21st Century Quality

When Greg Halling was hired at the *Elkhart (Indiana) Truth* in 2006, he wrote on his LinkedIn account: "I manage a small, nimble newsroom that generates content for online and print—but above all else, I do local journalism in the service of a community that needs context, meaning, and a voice speaking on its behalf."

A few years later, Halling was promoted to editor, committed to producing good, local journalism. Under his tenure, the *Elkhart Truth* won numerous awards through the years, but it did particularly well at the 2015 Indiana Associated Press Media Editors competition. On a Friday night in April, the *Truth* received 17 awards, including the Kent Cooper Award, which is IAPME's top honor, for a project titled "5 Years Later." The three-part series examined how the Great Recession affected the Elkhart community five years after the region led the nation in unemployment.

But on the night the newspaper received some of its highest accolades, Halling did not attend the ceremony. He had been "let go" by the *Elkhart Truth* a few months earlier. Halling was unemployed that night in April, still searching for a new newspaper job. "It hurt; I'm not going to lie about that. It stung," Halling said in 2016. "When you can build a team of like-minded journalists and they all share the same purpose of serving the needs of the community, the awards just kind of follow. The key is to find those people that have that fire and have that passion. For about two years, that newsroom was just magic."

The magic for Halling ended in mid-February 2015. The family-owned Truth Publishing company (the Dille family has owned the newspaper since the early 1950s) decided to restructure. During the restructuring, Halling and Publisher Brandon Erlacher were ousted. After guiding the *Elkhart Truth* through the Great Recession, implementing a digital-first format, and being recognized for producing good journalism, ownership decided it wasn't enough. "They decided they didn't want to pursue the same strategy that we had followed," Halling said. "They wanted to cut costs and try to save their way to prosperity. There's very little left of that newsroom. It is sad to reflect on but you look back and go, 'Man, we had a great run and we did absolutely vital work and we had fun doing it.'"

Producing good journalism is the stock-and-trade of newspapers. Good journalism equals good business. Previous research has shown that investment in the newsroom is associated with perceptions of producing quality journalism, enhances circulation and, in turn, creates more advertising revenue. When newsroom investment diminishes, and layoff survivors are asked to absorb the additional workload, quality is likely to change.

Defining journalistic quality is a tenuous endeavor, and has previously been reliant upon grading scales, (Rosenstiel, Gottlieb, and Brady, 2000; PEJ, 2003), ratings and awards (Spavins, Denison, Roberts, and Frenette, 2002), and newsroom investment (more investment equals commitment to quality) (Scott, Gobetz, and Chanslor, 2008). Some have argued that quality is not defined by what is being produced properly but by what is not being produced properly (Picard, 2000). For instance, typos, poor grammar, and factual errors would be elements of poor journalistic quality. Does that then deem clean copy and accurate reporting of facts to be good journalism? What of the context of the information or fairness in reporting? Picard (2000) wrote, "The quality concept is problematic when applied to journalism because it is nearly impossible to articulate what elements make up the concept" (p. 97).

Interviews with nearly 100 newsroom journalists revealed a growing concern that the reduction in staff and increase in work demands was depleting the quality of journalism. The problem is multidimensional. Time to produce solid, multiple-sourced, fact-checked stories has been condensed. Developing content for multiple platforms creates a "robbing Peter to pay Paul" scenario. When audience and online analytics drive content decisions, the journalism of today is not the journalism quality of yesterday.

Quality for Quality's Sake

Journalism is a product no different than car tires, pork rinds, or widgets. And as with all commodities, the quality of the work determines success. In 2004, *Newspaper Research Journal* attempted to tackle the difficult confluence of journalism quality and business success. In its issue "Good Journalism, Good Business," *NRJ* special editors Stephen Lacy, Esther Thorson, and John Russial (2004) concluded that newsroom investment enhanced the quality of journalism being produced, and ultimately improved financial performance. Nonetheless, Lacy et al., acknowledged the opposite was occurring. Some newspaper managers were content on mining short-term profits at the expense of long-term consequences, consequences that would not occur until long after those managers had departed. "Some newspaper companies have extracted high profits through disinvestment in newsrooms," they wrote: "Concern about profit-driven management has led to meetings among industry observers and calls to industry leaders to reinvest in their newsrooms not just to serve the public but to maintain the financial performance and long-term health of their companies" (p. 2).

The divestment in newsrooms has drained its most valuable commodity – newsroom staff. Newspapers have, in effect, fed on their seed corn by repeatedly depleting their journalists through layoffs and attrition. Simultaneously, workloads with online and social media obligations, along with merging job responsibilities created by the departures, compound the problem. As demonstrated throughout this book, the dedicated staffers who remain are burning out, are experiencing heavy workloads, and are not receiving the necessary support to fulfill the newspaper's mission.

However, research here also shows job satisfaction in newsrooms has stabilized following a time of disruption. Newspaper journalists continue to take great pride in their profession. They are committed to the newspaper's holistic community mission of watchdog, informer, storyteller, and supporter of social issues. But in an environment where "working harder and faster" is the mantra, sustaining a high quality of work is not probable.

In the *NJR* issue "Good Journalism, Good Business," Rosenstiel and Mitchell (2004) examined 1987 Inland Press Association data involving dozens of newspapers, in an attempt to locate indicators of newspaper quality and the outcomes of quality. At the time, newspapers had cut about 2,000 positions between 1990 and 2004, leaving Rosenstiel and Mitchell to note the increased workloads caused by staff reductions. During the next 10 years, newsroom losses grew to nearly 20,000 journalists.

Researchers in 2004 started to speculate that newspaper owners, even perhaps unknowingly, were liquidating their businesses in what Rosenstiel and Mitchell (2004) suggested was a suicide spiral. As circulation and advertising revenue declined, newspapers cut costs—i.e. newsroom staff—to reconcile the balance sheet. When that failed, the cycle was perpetuated. They wrote, "These cuts subtly reduce the quality and breadth of the paper. That, in turn, alienates readers, which then adds further pressure on circulation and advertising, which in turn leads to further cuts in costs, and the cycle spirals on" (p. 87).

In their study, Rosenstiel and Mitchell (2004) reported that investment in the newsroom budget had a positive impact on overall revenues. Investment in personnel, more newshole, or travel improved the product and ultimately revenues. However, investment risk-reward outcomes are a long-term proposition and probably would not result in immediate profits. Rosenstiel and Mitchell wrote: "But—and this is a crucial point—all the other indicators suggest that over time a newspaper will drive up both circulation and revenue and increase profit" (p. 94).

Clearly the newspaper landscape has changed since 2004. The Internet makes the newspaper newshole an antiquated concept. Audiences are splintered and self-select their news. Journalists now carry new obligations that were unforeseen in 2004—social media, continuous deadlines, unrelenting competition. Nonetheless, quality based upon the traditional journalistic tenets of truth, reliability, facts, and fairness remains a valued commodity readers expect.

The 2013 State of the News Media report revealed that 31 percent of news consumers had abandoned a particular news outlet "because it no longer provides the news and information they had grown accustomed to" (Enda and Mitchell, 2013). Additionally, those most likely to leave their media outlets were better educated, wealthier, and older than those who did not—in other words, they are people who tend to be most prone to consume and pay for news" (Enda and Mitchell, 2013).

By 2015, newspaper circulation had fallen by 19 percent, and advertising revenue was down by about 50 percent. With fewer than 37,000 journalists, newsrooms were at their lowest level since the mid-1970s (Barthel, 2015). And along with all the additional responsibilities of producing news, staffers at times were asked to deliver the paper as well. Delivery problems persisted after the *Orange County Register* and *Boston Globe* switched carriers. To solve the problem, both newspapers asked newsroom staff to assist with delivery (Khouri, 2014; Stelter, 2016).

Smaller workforce, more work, and new, different work prompted the reality that something had to give. After studying the digital transformation of a newspaper newsroom, Suzanne Robinson (2011) wrote: "At stake in these newsroom transformations is the quality of journalism in the United States, as more newspapers announce they are 'going digital' by eliminating the daily newspaper in favor of online products" (p. 1,123).

Perception of Quality

I, too, struggled to define quality. The variety of subjective measurements in itself is loaded with inconsistency. Local and regional awards tell us that a newspaper won something, but what did it win? Was it the best of the worst among entrants? Did the work appeal to the whims and preferences of the contest judges? Although the judging is deemed anonymous, bias toward one newspaper or another can still occur.

Financial measurements of quality present other obstacles. Does an increase in circulation, or website and social media traffic, and advertising revenue equal a good quality newspaper? As previously mentioned, there is a correlation between quality and long-term fiscal viability; however, monetary gain does not define good journalism. Financial prosperity might not be a result of good journalism, but other issues such as loyal readership, breaking news, or a subscription drive. For instance, a story about the fire department rescuing a cat from a storm drain can draw tons of online traffic, but is it good journalism?

Scientifically, measuring quality presents a cadre of other problems. Examining content, for example, hinges upon what is examined and how it is being measured. Do good leads define quality? But what constitutes a good lead? Does the study examine the extent of community coverage? Or, source selection used in stories? What about spelling and grammar, or number of corrections the newspaper posts?

Mostly researchers have avoided wading into the tumultuous waters of defining newspaper journalistic quality. For my 2014 study, I approached quality from one direction using two different methods. Both allowed news-room staffers the autonomy to determine quality. Journalists were asked about their perceptions of their paper's work, comparing the current work to previous work. The self-critique placed the onus on journalists to define and evaluate quality.

In terms of method, I developed a statistical measurement that included five survey questions. The questions included such items as "My newspaper is committed to producing good journalism," "I sacrifice work quality to get the job finished," (reverse coded) and "The work we do now is better than when I started here." Journalists were asked to respond on a seven-point scale from strongly disagree to strongly agree. A reliability analysis determined that the results can be reproduced 80 percent of the time. In essence, the measurement is considered scientifically dependable, stable, and consistent.

The second method used to determine quality was face-to-face interviews with nearly 100 daily newspaper journalists. The journalists were asked, "How would you characterize the quality of your newspaper?" Combined, the two measurements provided a unique perspective into journalists' impression of work quality at their newspapers.

Quality Journalism Today

More than 1,500 respondents completed the "Quality Section" of the 2014 survey. The overall mean score of perceived quality was 2.96 out of a possible 7. On the 1 = strongly disagree to 7 = strongly agree scale, 3 rates as "slightly disagree" in terms of producing high quality work.

When examining what benefits work quality, a correlation analysis determined job satisfaction and support from the organization were positive influences. Negative influences included work overload, and burnout's exhaustion and cynicism variables. The perception of work quality among journalists experiencing classic burnout (high exhaustion and cynicism) was 2.4 out of 7.

There were no differences between men and women in terms of the perception of work quality. Among age groups, the 30-and-younger group had the highest quality rating (3.2 out of 7), and the 41-to-50-year-old group had the lowest (2.8). As for job title, copy editors had the lowest perception of quality (2.7) and managers had the higher perception (3.3).

Managers, particularly editors and managing editors, are expected to put a good face on the quality issue regardless of the reality. But some recognized quality news work had a different standard today. Tom was a long-time, well-respected editor at his mid-sized newspaper. He had committed more than three decades of his life to the newsroom, working his way to deputy editor when we spoke. Tom was an optimistic and encouraging boss, and well-liked throughout his newsroom. But even Tom realized the paper wasn't producing at the same level of quality as it once had. He said the paper's quality was "still pretty high" but there were holes.

> What we're missing is good depth. I don't think the quality of depth is there like we used to have. I think our front-line quality is pretty good. What we don't have is much depth inside the paper. We don't have as much ability to peel people off for even a week and say, "Work on this story for a week and we'll see if it's a story or not." Now, if we peel you off for a week, it has to be a story. We don't have a week to explore. When we go fishing we want to catch some sort of fish.

When examining the statistical data, the glaringly noticeable commonality of the results was that the perception of quality among all the groups hovered near the "slightly disagree" response. In fact, of the 1,517 respondents, only 253 (17 percent) registered a score of 4 (neither disagree or agree) or higher on the perception of work quality variable.

Two overriding themes emerged in the interviews. One, the workload was so intense that making that extra call to a source, taking additional time to fact check, and producing clean copy were sacrificed. Two, creating stories that generated online traffic compromised story selection and input versus output rewards.

Thirty-one-year-old Giles was working at his small daily newspaper for less than two years. He talked about a Sunday centerpiece story that needed to be completed while trying to maintain his daily work responsibilities. "It was a short week for me because I was on vacation," he said. "I ran out of time during the week and worked on it from my parent's house. A lot of it is the demand of what we need to do to fill the paper. Sometimes I'm not too keen on it but I understand it. A lot of time it depends on what our needs are for the paper."

Even during Giles' short time at the newspaper the objectives had changed. The reporters were encouraged to write shorter stories, and produce more copy. Management encouraged generating clicks, posting daily Web traffic reports that celebrated those who produced the most clicks. Giles was becoming discouraged, saying that the journalism he was asked to produce wasn't nearly as rewarding as the journalism he wanted to produce.

> It's slightly disturbing. We get the stats every day about the most read stories and it's a tree limb falling on a guy or some bicyclist getting hit or a guy breaking into (the local grocery story) and falling through the ceiling that gets the most hits. Mine aren't heavily read online because they are more in-depth. I told this to my editor – I get more feedback with people picking up the phone and calling after reading it in print than online kind of feedback.

Within two months of the interview, Giles left that newspaper to become a reporter at mid-sized daily.

Newspaper journalists have always assumed tremendous responsibility when developing news content. Determining what is newsworthy, finding the right sources for a story, locating an assembly of stakeholders to provide a variety of perspectives, and deciding who receives a voice in the story and who doesn't fall to the reporters, editors, and copy editors. Now, additional considerations include online appeal, Web traffic generation, and digital media audiences. Traditional reporting conducted under more generous deadlines—hours instead of minutes—afforded more thorough reporting. Never-ending, 24/7 deadlines create a journalism of immediacy and sensationalism.

And generational differences cannot be ignored. Baby Boomers, Gen-X, and Gen-Y all work differently. A litany of research has shown work values vary, particularly between Baby Boomers (born 1946–1964) and Gen-Y (1978–1990). While Boomers value "hard work," Gen-Y values "leisure" (Cogin, 2012), expect superiors to provide instant feedback, and want to receive constant approval (Cennamo and Gardner, 2008; Lowe, Levitt, and Wilson, 2008; Reynolds, Bush, and Geist, 2008; Gibson, Greenwood, and Murphy, 2009; Aruna and Anitha, 2015). Immediate gratification and work rewards motivate Gen Y as they work for more work-life balance than previous generations, and equate hard work to personal and professional success (Cogin, 2012). Aruna and Anitha (2015) wrote:

> As Gen Y tend to behave more like investors than assets, seeking the best return on their investment of time and energy with an employer, it is high time that the management had to redesign the organisational processes, structure and methods according to the style and approach of Gen Y (p. 9).

Some newsrooms have adapted to the Gen Y mindset at the detriment of producing high quality journalism. Developing quick-hit stories that drive

Web traffic is time efficient with immediate rewards. Chasing clicks, and driving social media traffic emboldens a generation already intent on earning praise from the boss. It reinforces the idea that quick-and-easy journalism is good journalism, and perpetuates routines journalistically counterintuitive to producing high quality work. Newsroom Web reports supplemented with management praise can serve to discourage diligent, time-consuming reporting. Staffers find additional reinforcement of quick-and-quirky stories from a public that would much rather read about a woman who tried to shoot the bunion off her foot with a 38-special than the city commission's plans to raise property taxes.

Few newsroom staffers said the quality of their newspaper work was poor. Instead, 65 percent of the staffers said the quality of the newspaper was not as good as it once was. "The paper has had a tremendous drop in quality," said Troy, a 48-year-old news editor at a mid-sized daily. "It's not that there's no individual out there that isn't doing the best work they can do but they're either being pulled into multiple directions … or they are being asked to multitask in different ways such as collect video or audio for the Web or just take on an additional beat."

Matt, a 35-year-old crime reporter at a mid-sized newspaper, expressed similar concerns.

> I mean overall, yeah, the quality has declined. On a personal level, it isn't like I don't strive to do the same type of work or better work that I've done in the past but there are too many things in the pipeline to feel like you can make the extra effort. Not only give your story a little more oomph but also help you cultivate a relationship with someone that can lead to more different and better stories down the line.

After more than a decade at his small daily, Chad's coverage of local government and business earned him the title of senior reporter. The staff had seen its share of reductions, but the paper still maintained prominence and respect in the community. At 42 and a senior statesman in what had become a much younger newsroom because of cuts, Chad recognized the shifting tide of news work. "The quality is different. I write many more one-source stories than I used to," he said. "Maybe it wasn't efficient in the old days. Sometimes you felt like you needed two people in the story and sometimes you were talking to someone who wasn't giving you a whole helluva lot but you have to have a name in there. There's really no question when you do that anymore. Before there was an expectation and there is not anymore."

In reporting stories, Chad said his experience allowed him to determine how stories were sourced and when an extra interview was needed. But he also admitted sourcing decisions today were based on different parameters than a few years ago. He said if he is confident one source provided the basic elements of a story, he will not take time to interview a second source.

Quality, Chad said, was different than in years past. Loss of institutional and community knowledge played a role as much as audience expectations and digital obligations. But in the end, he realized, the newsroom culture had changed. "Anytime you squeeze productivity to the point we've squeezed it, quality has to be a concern ... The productivity squeeze to me has squeezed a lot of the culture out of the place. You've just got to get your shit done."

For newspaper staffers who do not have the institutional knowledge, the quality issue is a foreign concept. For the 30 and younger journalists and veteran journalists, the chasm of what defines good journalism is vast. When discussing quality, Patty, a 30-year-old reporter at mid-sized newspaper said:

> Although we're doing a lot more with a lot less, I truly believe the quality has improved. I think we are working harder than ever and trying to be more innovative than ever. I look at the paper now compared to when I first started or four or five years ago, I think it's edgier, a better looking product.

As a 24-year-old city reporter at another mid-sized newspaper, Laura had a similar take. "I would say that our good stuff is really good," she said. "When we've had reporters who can investigate and get in-depth into stories, we've had some really awesome pieces of journalism. That kind of work I'm really proud of and I think most of the people in the newsroom agree."

At 50, Nick had worked in that same newsroom for half his life. As a reporter, he had a different take than Laura, who was in her second year at the paper.

> The quality of reporting and writing is just not going to be as good. When you're focused on one story a day or maybe have a couple of days to work on something, I think it really shows. Right now it seems everyone is really rushing from one thing to the next. I don't think the quality is what it was. Relative to everybody else in the business I think it's good but in general everything has gone down.

Conclusions

After Greg Halling left the *Elkhart Truth*, he moved west to again rebuild a newspaper with great community journalism suited for the 21st century. A couple months after the 2015 Indiana Associated Press Media Editors competition, Halling became the *Ogden, Utah, Standard-Examiner* editor. Elkhart's former publisher Brandon Erlacher joined Halling in Utah as well, along with three other former Elkhart staffers. In Utah, Halling said they strive to replicate the quality journalism and community service they had provided in Indiana.

Still, even after a year out of the Elkhart newsroom, Halling reminisces about what his team had created in a struggling community during a time it needed a good newspaper most. "I never doubted that I was right and (ownership) was wrong," he said. "The work that we did was work that needed to be done and there's a continuing need for the journalism that we did.

"I feel bad for the community that I left behind because there's clearly a different perception of the need for journalism in Elkhart than when I was there. But if you're a newspaper that's happy to return a tidy profit and that's what's important to you, then great, you should be that newspaper. But in my mind newspapers are built to accomplish something. Elkhart needed us. We had an obligation to that community."

Halling is not alone in his convictions. Generally, journalists are committed to producing good journalism but extenuating circumstances in the early part of the century have proven to be obstacles. And, those producing the work have acknowledged that the journalism of today is not of the same standard as the journalism of yesterday.

Of course, work quality takes on several definitions and perspectives, none of which truly capture an all-encompassing meaning. Personal tastes, organizational standards, generational expectations, and shifting work demands contribute to the notions of creating good quality work.

Here, the research allowed journalists to determine their own perceptions of quality. Newsroom workers were asked to compare and critique their own work. They sat in judgment of the journalism being produced today, and generally concluded that the labor-intensive initiatives expected of a diminishing number of staffers was taking its toll on the end product. Instead of producing great work, "good enough" was becoming the high-water mark to meet the demands of continuous online deadlines that increased website visits.

Further compounding the problem was a management staff that posted and praised the reporters driving online analytics, perpetuating a Pavlov-like reaction from a generation accustomed to immediate gratification and praise. For some young newspaper journalists who did not have a point of historical reference, quick-and-easy stories were classified as quality journalism. The culture of tracking down three good sources to produce depth and perspective in a story was unfamiliar to a Y Generation newsroom. And while it drew consternation from the veterans, there was no time to properly indoctrinate the young journalists into what was a long-held standard of quality. Besides, respected managers, who measured audience not by circulation but by Web analytics, rewarded the production of quick-and-easy stories.

That isn't to say Gen Y journalists are not inclined to produce good journalism. They are, but not at the same benchmarks as previous generations. Simply put, the overall expectation of quality has shifted. For journalists 30-and-younger, the new reality of quality is their accepted standard. It's all they've known. The loss of veteran news workers depleted institutional values and knowledge. The stalwarts who held the line on producing good work based on the traditional journalistic tenets of truth, reliability, facts, and fairness are either gone or too busy to instill the old standard.

Even for veterans who said quality work continues to churn from their newsrooms, the comments came with a caveat – the quality is good under the circumstances. In the foreseeable future the circumstances that halved the size of newsrooms and expanded workloads are expected to warrant an asterisk whenever the new generation of news workers discuss their idea of good journalism. And if those producing the work have seen a decline in quality, surely those reaching for the newspaper or clicking onto the website see a decline as well. If history tells us anything about consumers and products, quality matters.

References

Aruna, M., and Anitha, J. (2015). Employee retention enablers: Generation Y employees. *SCMS Journal of Indian Management*, July-September: 94–103.

Barthel, M. (2015). Newspaper fact sheet. *State of the News Media 2015*. Pew Research Center, April 29. www.journalism.org/files/2015/04/FINAL-STATE-OF-THE-NEWS-MEDIA1.pdf.

Cogin, J. (2012). Are generational differences in work values fact or fiction? Multi-country evidence and implications. *The International Journal of Human Resource Management*, 23(11): 2268–94.

Cennamo, L. and Gardner, D. (2008). Generational differences in work values, outcomes and person-organizational values fit. *Journal of Managerial Psychology*, 23: 891–906.

Enda, J. and Mitchell, A. (2013). Americans show signs of leaving a news outlet, citing less information. *The State of the News Media 2013*. Pew Research Center, April. http://stateofthemedia.org/2013/special-reports-landing-page/citing-reduced-quality-many-americans-abandon-news-outlets/.

Gibson, J., Greenwood, R., and Murphy, E. (2009). Generational differences in the workplace: Personal values, behaviours, and popular beliefs. *Journal of Diversity Management*, 4(3): 1–7.

Khouri, A. (2014). O.C. Register asks reporters to help deliver its newspapers. *Los Angeles Times*, November 14. www.latimes.com/business/la-fi-register-deliveries-20141114-story.html.

Lacy, S., Thorson, E., and Russial, J. (2004). Special issue editors' comments. *Newspaper Research Journal*, 25(1): 1–5.

Lowe, D., Levitt, K., and Wilson, T. (2008). Solutions for retaining Generation Y employees in the workplace. *Business Renaissance Quarterly*, 3(3): 43–57.

PEJ Project (2003). Does ownership matter in local television news: A five-year study of ownership and quality. Project for Excellence in Journalism, April 29. www .journalism.org/2003/04/29/which-ownership-produces-the-best-quality-news/.

Picard, R.G. (2000). *Measuring media content, quality, and diversity: Approaches and issues in content research*. Turku, Finland: Turku School of Economics and Business Administration Business Research and Development Centre.

Reynolds, L., Bush, E.C., and Geist, R. (2008). The Gen Y imperative. *Communication World:* 25(2): 19–22.

Robinson, S. (2011). Convergence crises: News work and news space in the digitally transforming newsroom. *Journal of Communication*, 61: 1122–41.

Rosenstiel, T., Gottlieb, C., and Brady, L.A. (2000). Local TV news project 1999: Quality brings higher ratings, but enterprise is disappearing. *Project for Excellence in Journalism*, March 1. www.journalism.org/node/387.

Rosenstiel, T. and Mitchell, A. (2004). The impact of investing in newsroom sources. *Newspaper Research Journal*, 25(1): 84–97.

Scott, D.K., Gobetz, R.H., and Chanslor, M. (2008). Chain versus independent television station ownership: Toward an investment model of commitment to local news quality. *Communication Studies*, 59(1): 84–98.

Spavins, T.C., Denison, L., Roberts, S., and Frenette, J. (2002). The measurement of local television news and public affairs programs. Federal Communications Commission, Sept. 1. www.fcc.gov/working-papers/measurement-local-television-news-and-public-affairs-programs.

Stelter, B. (2016). Paper routes for a night: *Boston Globe* reporters deliver Sunday's edition. *CNN Money*, January 3. http://money.cnn.com/2016/01/02/media/boston-globe-reporters-deliver-sunday/.

8 The Next Generation

In more than 100 years of family ownership, through two world wars, a Great Depression, and recessions in the 1970s and 1980s, publishers at Henry's mid-sized daily newspaper boasted that they had never initiated layoffs. The ownership featured a diverse portfolio of media entities, but the flagship newspaper remained its gemstone and most profitable.

In 1999, with a circulation between 50,001–100,000, the newsroom employed 91 full-time staffers. But in 2008, at the heart of the housing crisis and recession that followed, Henry's paper did the unthinkable—it offered voluntary buyouts. By 2016, buyouts and attrition had reduced Henry's news staff to 57.

Henry dedicated his life to the newspaper, working his way from a cub reporter to executive editor in a span of 30 years. He was committed to hyper-local community journalism, understood new digital audiences, and continued to respect and accommodate an aging readership. In subsequent years following the downsizing, Henry and his staff re-evaluated the newspaper's mission. They took an inventory of coverage needs and available resources for filling the needs. Tough decisions followed as the paper withdrew from fringe coverage areas where readership was stable but advertising revenue was not.

"I'm not necessarily saying that's a good idea because I think the loss in circulation coincides with that loss in hyper-local news in those areas," Henry said in 2016. "But the truth of the matter is there isn't big business outside there. There's not a whole lot of dollars at risk but readership is at risk."

Henry pushed his staff to embrace online and social media initiatives, invested in technology as needed, hired a digital analytics expert, and financed readership and customer studies. Still, his paper faced a conundrum. Even with downsizing, the coverage modifications and technological investments, the paper continued to operate at a profit margin between 20 and 25 percent. In comparison, the average profit margin of a supermarket is between 1 and 3 percent (Huebsch, 2016). "None of the proprieties are even close to not being profitable," Henry said. "It's a double-edged sword for us because of that we're still extremely print focused. Our discussions still start with print and at some point you have to migrate that but you don't want to jump the gun because you have so much money at stake.

"Every day I attempt to bring more online discussion into the operation. There's not a whole lot of feeling we need to do something rapidly. We're making pennies on the Web and dollars on print."

Research from Henry's news staff showed that while the burnout rate was similar to the national sample, the perception of the quality of journalism being produced was substantially higher than other newspapers of similar size. Also, Henry's staff reported high rates of job satisfaction and support from the organization – both above the national sample and sample of other mid-sized newspapers. The newspaper's staff workload rates were no different than other journalists. But when asked, "How would you characterize the quality of your newspaper?" Eighty-nine percent of journalists in Henry's newsroom said it was good or better than it was in the past. In the national sample, only 35 percent answered the question with a positive response.

Allocation of Resources

As an employee gains work experience and becomes indoctrinated into an organizational environment, he or she becomes more efficient and skilled at doing the work. Good and bad experiences prepare workers to be better equipped to manage unforeseen problems. Over time, workers accumulate a deep well of resources, particularly with everyday tasks. For instance, a veteran cops reporter is better suited to cover a crime scene than a novice. The cop reporter knows what sources to interview at the scene, can anticipate information that will be available, and how to negotiate on and off the record materials with police. The cops reporter also knows how quickly a story needs to be turned, and if information is limited, how to track down police reports and jail logs. His experience allows him to manage the stress and navigate roadblocks along the way.

Employees work to gain and defend what they value, and during stressful times will try to retain valued resources, which can include "objects, personal characteristics, conditions, or energies that are valued by the individual" and include "mastery of a skill, self-esteem, learned resourcefulness, socioeconomic status and employment" (Hobfoll, 1989, p. 516).

During a time of crisis, workers tap into their reserve of resources to maintain a high quality of work. However, losses are more relevant than gains, so stressful situations are compounded when resources are threatened, lost, or are invested but fail to provide satisfactory outcomes. Stockpiled resources, then, help counter stress. For example, if the copy desk cuts three workers, the remaining employees are required to pick up the slack. Because the remaining copy editors have years of experience, the additional workload might be manageable but more mistakes might be made, which in turn reduces the copy editors' level of work satisfaction. As satisfaction falls, stress increases and the cycle continues at a downward spiral. So, if workers invest time and energy or other resources into a project, and the project fails to meet expectations, resources have been lost, which only further exasperates an already disgruntled workforce.

Other threats to an employee's reserve of resources include possible layoffs, or risks to financial stability or self-esteem. Repeated layoffs keep workers on edge, as does the possibility of furloughs or wage cuts. Self-esteem is lost when a worker does not feel valued or the work he or she is doing is not valued. Behavioral Science Professor and renowned stress researcher Stevan Hobfoll (1989) wrote:

> This discussion begs the question of what people employ to offset resource loss or to gain resources. The answer to this question is that they employ resources that they possess or they call on resources available to them from their environment. Individuals, for instance, invest their love and affection to receive a return of the same. Often individuals invest their time and energy, two important resources, in attempt to translate them to other more highly prized resources, for example, power and money (p. 517).

If resources are depleted or threatened, additional negative outcomes can occur, such as burnout and job dissatisfaction (Taris, Schreurs, and Schaufeli, 1999). The same can happen when a worker invests resources but the return on the investment falls short of expectations (Taris et al., 1999). For instance, if a photographer isn't able to complete an assignment, and the news editor says she'll cover for the missed assignment but doesn't, the photographer's stress is compounded. The results are the photographer's job satisfaction and commitment to the newspaper declines, as does his work quality (Karasek, Triantis, and Chaudhry, 1982; Yang and Carayon, 1995; Noblet, Rodwell, and McWilliams, 2006).

As the research here has shown, a decade of staff cuts, and increased workloads that include new and different digital work, has tapped veteran journalists of their resources. Because experienced workers had not acquired a reserve of resources in producing content for online and social media, stress was compounded, creating burnout and quality of work issues.

For 29 years, Mike had worked a variety of jobs at his mid-sized daily. At 53, he was a page editor who had grown cynical of his ownership's mission.

"I think the (newspaper's) mission is to sell as much advertising as possible, frankly. I think the product we sell as news is pretty much beside the point."

Mike had experienced the newspaper's heyday when the staff was twice as large and investigative journalism won them a cadre of awards and accolades from peers and readers. But in 2014, he said morale was as low as it had ever been. He said ownership had bled the paper for what it could financially, and quality work was rare. Additionally, Mike adopted a curmudgeon's view of the management's online initiatives. "We go out of our way to alienate our core readership, our customer base," he said. "All the emphasis is on the online product and time to lure young readers to the disadvantage to our senior readers. They're the ones who buy the paper."

Mike's perceptions weren't uncommon among career newsroom journalists. Many discussed how their newspapers rolled out digital initiations without purpose. News staffs were told to blog, but were never told why. Then they were told to Facebook, but weren't sure how that made the newspaper better. Twitter, Tumblr, Snapchat, Pinterest, and on and on. No journalistic or financial plan was explained or implemented. They were simply told to, "drive Web traffic."

News staffs became disillusioned as valuable resources were expended without a clearly defined purpose. The unintended consequence was that the good work previously created by a dedicated veteran staff was slipping. Staff trust was lost and the product suffered.

Chad, a 43-year-old news editor with 15 years experience at his mid-sized daily summed it up for many:

> The website becomes like a giant newspaper. If we can fit it there, the conversation is, "Dump it on the Web," which immediately marginalizes it. So instead of being an important place where we want to drive people it becomes a dumping ground, and that's the mentality that a lot of people have. If you actually want to convince people the website is important you have to devote resources to it.

For young journalists who did not have a resource reserve developed through experiences, the perspective was much different. They were not shackled by long-held institutional beliefs. A shift in the resources paradigm for the veterans was not a shift at all for the novices. More, quicker, engage the audience was all they knew from their newsroom experiences. When those under 30 were asked about their newspaper's online mission, they said it was to post stories as quickly as possible, drive traffic to different audiences, and engage on social media. Although those were the general marching orders in most newsrooms, the veterans wondered to what end, and struggled to follow through. Meanwhile, the under-30 crowd not only had a clearer understanding of the purpose but embraced it.

Nick started his career at a small newspaper that was known for its progressive online work. After a couple years as a copy editor, at 25 Nick was named the paper's first digital editor. He embraced the position but quickly realized he was the bridge between the old guard and the new. Nick respected the veteran staff and boasted of the good work they did. However, he saw the future and it wasn't the traditional doorstep newspaper. "A mindset is one of the obstacles, especially in the newsroom," he said. "I'm guilty of it, too, coming from mostly the print side of things. The reporters, copy editors and editors, everyone needs to think more about the future and where those things are going than just the print side of things."

Meanwhile, Nick's managers pressured staff to generate online traffic. The newsroom Web traffic board and daily online reports were constant reminders that the Web needed to be fed. And, as the veteran staff mildly grumbled about the daily memos, the young staff embraced them. Nick said:

> There are pressures in the newsroom and traffic. Analytics are important and stressed at times, which is a good thing. I think we should be paying attention to those things to see what the community wants. But I also think there's a danger to do things only because of the traffic. You have to look outside that box at times to see what to cover and not cover.

Nick said there was a world where good journalism and online demands co-exist. Digital options afford for more and different types of stories, he said, but he certainly does not want his newsroom to abandon the good, investigative work in exchange for clicks. "Attempting to be all things to all people is not sustainable, even with an enormous staff," Nick said. "The same can be said for catering to clickbait while attempting to provide news of importance. But catering to clicks generated by stories of importance and interest provide a manifest for successful news development. Capturing that formula is contingent on the holistic understanding of the community."

With a decade more experience than Nick, Ted, 39, was the Web editor for his mid-sized newspaper. Similar to Nick, Ted was designated to be the bridge builder between journalism generations. Ted's staff was older than Nick's and had been working on the transition for a couple years. "Even the people who haven't completely embraced it have embraced more than they did before," Ted said. "I think the people who have embraced it have been a positive influence on those who have not. Those who haven't embraced it, there have been some missed opportunities."

Ted's newsroom also had a Web board prominently posted in the newsroom but it did not receive the attention that the board in Nick's newsroom had. But, Ted said, when staff saw the Web traffic reports it was a wakeup call.

Being able to see the reaction of people online – user comments, analytics – that has really aided in seeing what the audience, the community, the customers find important and interesting. There seems to be less boring, stale stuff. More than ever, people are thinking about what extras we can put online – documents, video, and breaking news we can update continuously.

Making It Work

Remember Greg Halling from Chapter 7? Halling spent years redesigning and developing an award-winning, digital-first newsroom in Elkhart, Indiana. While in Elkhart during the height of recession, Halling reorganized the newsroom. Control of the website moved from IT into the newsroom, where journalists assumed full responsibility of online content. Halling and his staff took an inventory of what they were covering, redesigned coverage needs, and allocated resources accordingly. "I'd like to think we were doing good journalism prior to 2008 and the Great Recession," Halling said. "The Great Recession gave us no choice. We had to re-examine everything we were doing because unemployment in Elkhart was 23 percent, people were in pain, our company was taking a financial hit, and we still had to figure out how to do good journalism on behalf of the broader community. We couldn't do things the same way that we had done them."

Following layoffs and buyouts, Halling hired younger journalists to assist in the cultural transformation, creating a newsroom of veterans with institutional and community knowledge, and novices with new media skills. Throughout the evolution, Halling learned two basic lessons: 1. Fearlessly pursue continuous innovation; 2. Force journalists to be engaged in the community.

> When journalists get comfortable they have a tendency to hunker down and withdraw from the community. You don't have that luxury when you're covering a community in crisis or you're a newsroom in crisis. You have to force journalists out into the community to encounter people where they live, find those stories, bring those stories back and tell them.

By 2013, Halling and his staff had turned the corner, but taking his own advice, he knew they needed to innovate. He developed a separate digital staff that worked alongside the traditional staff, and beefed up the online resources. "We built a real-time desk. We pulled a coder and designer into the newsroom who otherwise would have lived in the IT department. It made us more nimble, more affective, more responsive."

Halling was "let go" in 2015 after the family ownership restructured the news staff. Similar to the Mormons his newspaper in Ogden, Utah, covers, Halling migrated west to rebuild his vision of good newspapering at the *Standard-Examiner*. After hiring three former Elkhart staffers to join his dedicated, passionate Ogden staff, Halling was confident they could replicate the award-winning journalism in Utah that they had created in Indiana. However, there were challenges.

> There is good talent here but the newsroom was built upon a print product. It wasn't nimble and it had no digital focus. Those are tools if you know how to use them you can convert pretty quickly. It's a community that needs its newspaper. It's a community where the newspaper hadn't been very responsive or connected to the community for years. It was an inward looking newspaper and in need of transformation. The community is hungry for an involved newspaper. Have I found the Promised Land, yeah, I think I have.

Of course, for Halling or any editor to succeed, support of the publisher and ownership group is necessary. Newsroom management needs to be afforded the autonomy and patience to innovate and engage. A blended staff of young and veteran journalists is essential in maintaining the paper's historical standards of good journalism while moving into the digital age. "We have a good mix and it's still changing," Halling said of Ogden. "We couldn't be all of one or all of the other. We couldn't have gone with the newsroom that I inherited when I arrived because it didn't have the digital skills, the digital tools, and the willingness to embrace them. By the same token, if I brought in an entire newsroom of young newcomers we wouldn't understand the community as well as we do. It's a good blend."

The Future

In *The Human Equation*, author Jeffrey Pfeffer (1998) asks:

> When you look at your people, do you see costs to be reduced? Do you see recalcitrant employees prone to opportunism, shirking, and free riding who can't be trusted and who need to be closely controlled through monitoring, rewards, and sanctions? … Or, when you look at your people, do you see intelligent, motivated, trustworthy individuals – the most critical and valuable strategic assets your organization can have? (p. 292).

Through layoffs, buyouts, and attrition, newspaper newsrooms substantially cut their staffs. Some of those staffs needed to be trimmed.

There was organizational fat. For those not committed to producing good work or willing to adapt to new work routines, their expiration date had long passed. But throughout this research the remaining news workers repeatedly insisted that those who remained in the newsroom were the best-of-the-best. They were committed to innovative, quality journalism for digital and print venues. Now, what management does with the remaining staff will determine the future of newspapers. Too often, newsrooms downsized staff but did not right-size work demands. The imbalance has been incredibly detrimental to news people as demonstrated by rising levels of burnout, feelings of being overloaded with work, and a decline in the perception of work quality.

My research was not simply casting stones from the ivory tower. It represents a reflection of what newspaper journalists had been saying, thinking, and feeling during the past decade of seismic change. Evidence showed that news people and the quality of work they created was in peril. Lacking a concise mission, journalists were burdened with heavy workloads, new and different work without training, and a reduction in resources. Short-term profitability had superseded to long-term vitality and the well-being of newsroom personnel.

Admittedly, I did not directly address the financial difficulties facing newspapers. Economics were never the focus of my research. As a newsroom sociologist, the intent was to examine the workers charged with making the transformation, and the impact that the transformation had on news people. Developing a one-size-fits all economic model is not practical or realistic. The economics of each news organization is fundamentally unique to its community and company.

Wholesale transformation and cultural change in any industry is difficult. Generational divides and inconcise expectations compound the difficulty created by shifting markets and migrating customers. Based upon this research conducted during the past decade, I offer suggestions to assist in adapting to the new era in newspapers.

1   Re-evaluate the newspaper's mission. The fundamental watchdog mission of a newspaper has not changed; however, the circumstances of implementing the mission has. The newspaper's mission statement does not need to be completely overhauled but supplemented to include new initiatives, such as digital work. The newsroom staff needs to be able to rally around a common cause. The mission statement is a good place to start. Take an inventory of what needs to be covered by the newspaper and what does not. Pull back from fringe areas that require a great deal of resources without much gain in terms of news value or profits. The workload has to be modified to fit the staff size. Judicious decisions must be made.

2   Invest in training and technology. Newsroom managers need to remove the mystery about initiatives such as blogging or tweeting. Other than driving online traffic, definitive objectives need to be established. Investment needs to be made in digital technology. Producing good online work only benefits a community when the community can efficiently receive it. A website that is poorly managed or an app that doesn't work only frustrates the readers and diminishes the work effort.

3   Initiate readership surveys, focus groups, data analytics, and other research to determine readers' wants and needs. These tools can assist in developing desirable content and assist in allocating resources. While the tools will not holistically determine news coverage, it will allow the news staff to have a better understanding of the readership.

4   Along with the entire news staff, develop realistic goals and a long-range strategy. The best decisions are not made in a vacuum of managers. The newspaper's well-being rests in the hands of the staff. Create universal ownership by inviting others into the conversation. Allowing the workers to have a substantial say in the work allows for better outcomes.

5   After a staff reorganization, clearly define individual work responsibilities. A workload reorganization is crucial when a staff has been restructured. Who will pick up the work left behind by the departed worker? How will work from beats be redistributed? Defining what work will be done by whom is essential in avoiding issues down the road.

6   Develop a newsroom culture of transformation. A blended newsroom of veterans and young journalists appears to be a viable, successful model for moving a newspaper forward. Maintaining community and newsroom cultural institutional knowledge is essential to producing good, quality journalism. A veteran news staff can instill the traditional expectations that have made the newspaper viable for decades. A young staff can assist in migrating good journalism onto 21st century delivery systems while providing the needs of the digital community. A blended generational newsroom can fulfill the needs of a multi-generational audience.

7   Engage the community. As Greg Halling said, journalists need to be involved in their communities to report on them. Work demands have to be designed to free reporters to move beyond the pale of official sources and breaking news.

8   Understand multiple audiences and multiple products. A newspaper is no longer just the dead-tree version that hits driveways and doorsteps. A newspaper needs to be a media center that customizes service to multiple audiences. This is not a revelation; however, news staff and management too often have failed to fully embrace the idea of product development and diversity.

The suggestions are not new or revolutionary. Successful small and mid-sized newspapers have already implemented many or all of the practices. Nonetheless, based upon the research, I thought it prudent to identify some of these effective measures.

Conclusions

For hundreds of years, U.S. newspapers have operated under the privileged protection of the First Amendment while accepting a social responsibility to inform, safeguard and question a community. Accepting modest pay and strenuous work demands, news workers remained committed to what many believed to be a higher societal calling. For the committed, the reward was in the work.

However, after a historical media shift, traditional newspapers struggled to remain relevant in their communities. The old economic model that hinged on column-inch advertising was obsolete. And while newspaper companies attempted to develop a new model for online revenue, financial sustainability was maintained through newsroom divestment.

Between 2007–2016, about 20,000 journalists were laid off, bought out, or simply left newspapers. The divestment in human capital had a devastating effect on the layoff survivors. Burnout rose, job satisfaction leveled off, workloads exponentially increased, and commitment to the organization plummeted. The perception of the quality of work being produced also declined. An overwhelming number of news workers admitted the work they produced was of lower quality than in the past.

Those who left newsrooms took with them cultural, institutional, and community knowledge. The newspaper brain drain shattered expectations and traditions long established by generations of news workers. Work demands were so great that veteran journalists didn't have the time or energy to indoctrinate new workers into the cultural norms. Managers implemented online and social media initiatives without providing clear objectives or instructions. "Drive Web traffic" was the rallying cry, which fell on deaf ears among many veteran journalists.

As online work was pushed, promoted, and praised, the historical values of good, multi-sourced reporting diminished. Instead, energy went into quick-and-quirky online items that could go viral. Not knowing any different, Generation Y easily adopted what veterans saw as a lower quality of work.

The newsroom culture was in a state of flux. During times of change, an organization will prepare for adaptations, implement changes, and then return to a state of stability. Some of the original cultural traditions will survive the transformation. That, too, is the case with newspapers. Newsrooms will continue to be a valuable resource for the community. Perhaps there will be less investigative, insightful, analytical journalism occurring in those newsrooms, but new and different journalism will emerge through digital technologies. Some of it will be good and some will not be so good. How is that different from newspaper journalism during the past couple hundred years?

As for journalism's lost generation, there are many. Those who no longer work in newspaper newsrooms after years of dedicated service are lost to the profession and took with them a great deal of talent and cultural continuity.

Veteran news workers who remain in newsrooms but failed or refused to accept the changing world of their work are lost as well. They have been left behind by a technology that is here to stay. They yearn for the "good old days" when working for the newspaper commanded respect, and the work they did fulfilled the community's needs.

And, the young journalists could, too, be lost. Without the guidance of a veteran staff to indoctrinate the culture and traditions of the past, Gen-Y is left to its own devices to decide what quality journalism means. For better or worse, they will drive the new newsroom culture. They understand digital content and audiences, and provide a fresh perspective to an industry that has been slow to innovate.

For more than a decade I have amassed scores of data and talked with hundreds journalists about their newspaper work. The results are a reflection of U.S. newspaper newsrooms during this tumultuous time in the industry. According to the *2016 Editor & Publisher Newspaper Databook of Dailies*, 96 percent of U.S. newspapers have circulations less than 100,000. Intentionally, my research focused on mid-sized and small newspapers.

This research, by no means, is a comprehensive examination of newspaper newsrooms. It's a point in time when changes are occurring at incredible speeds. However, it is important to recognize that many journalists in these newsrooms are on the brink of change. Some will adapt and continue to do great work. Others will not, and either be forced out of the newsroom or leave on their own. In the 21st century of newspaper journalism, a journalist doesn't just lose a job; he or she loses a career.

For all journalism generations, there needs to be an understanding that online and social media are merely new delivery systems for good content. "Man bites dog" always received great reader interest. The only difference now is that newsrooms can instantaneously post a video, Snapchat, or tweet about the offended dog. Content continues to be king. Good journalism equals good business. Without support from ownership and management, the newspaper's most valuable resource—its people—will wither away. Without dedicated news people serving the community, what might follow is a lost generation of informed citizens.

References

Editor & Publisher (2016). *95th annual newspaper databook of dailies.* Irvin, CA: Duncan McIntosh Co. Inc.

Hobfoll, S.E. (1989). Conservation of resources: A new attempt at conceptualizing stress. *American Psychologist*, 44(3): 513–24.

Huebsch, R. (2016). What is the average profit margin for a supermarket? Demand Media, http://smallbusiness.chron.com/profit-margin-supermarket-22467.html

Karasek, R., Triantis, K., and Chaudhry, S. (1982). Coworker and supervisor support as moderators of associations between task characteristics and mental strain. *Journal of Occupational Behavior*, 2: 181–200.

Noblet, A., Rodwell, J., and McWilliams, J. (2006). Organizational change in the public sector: Augmenting the demand control model to predict employee outcomes under New Public Management. *Work & Stress*, 20(4): 335–52.

Pfeffer, J. (1998). The human equation: Building profits by putting people first. Boston, Mass.: Harvard Business School Press.

Taris, T.W., Schreurs, P.J.G., and Schaufeli, W.B. (1999). Construct validity of the Maslach Burnout Inventory-General Survey: A two-sample examination of its factors structure and correlates. *Work & Stress*, 13(3): 223–37.

Yang C., and Carayon, P. (1995). Effect of job demands and social support on worker stress: A study of VDT users. *Behavior and Information Technology*, 14: 32–40.

Index